Thank you for being part of the #LeadWithGiants chat. May the insights shared in the event and in this book help in your journey to create or become part of a fearless front line!

Be you! Be fearless!

Praise for **The Fearless Front Line**
and Ray Attiyah

"Too many business books leave the reader thirsting for more detail as often they provide just a cursory overview of major themes. Ray instead drills down to cover the how, when, and why so that *The Fearless Front Line* actually becomes a workbook for implementing behavioral change. This is a must-have reference for those at the top of the organization through to shop floor personnel. If you are serious in making systemic improvement in your organization then this is an excellent blueprint that shows you the way."
—Jim Barney, president Belmont Advisory Group

"Not only is *The Fearless Front Line* fun to read, but it is powerful information that can be put to use on your business the same day you read it. Ray's insights are just awesome!
—Fabian A. Schmahl, president & CEO,
Thyssen Krupp Bilstein of America, Inc.

"The last book I read that moved me this much was *Good to Great*. Ray has given leaders a guide to move from their current state to world class—this is an amazing book. The Run-Improve-Grow (RIG) business model featured in *The Fearless Front Line* is presented with such clarity and has energized me to focus on our culture. This will be a great guide for me."
—Mike Collinsworth, president,
Custom Manufacturing Solutions, Inc.

"Ray Attiyah provides an inspirational and sound approach for leaders to drive out non-value-added work and create environments where people, innovation, and business can truly flourish."
—Cheri M. Stevenot, director of Global Research
and Development, Fortune 100 Company

"In this book, Ray Attiyah offers a refreshing way to think about improvement and growth by focusing on core processes and supervision. I firmly believe that Ray's prescription of relying on human assets is the formula that leads to magical transformations and sustainable competitive advantage. Ray demonstrates this principle in very persuasive way through many examples and cases. A must-read for any manager who is looking for ways to invest in human assets and front line supervision."

—Amitabh Raturi, professor of operations management,
Lindner College of Business, University of Cincinnati

"*The Fearless Front Line* offers excellent advice to businesses of all sizes and to employees throughout the organization chart—from the CEO on down. As a former manufacturing CEO, I respect the fact that Ray has actual hands-on experience running complex manufacturing businesses, which shows in his sound, practical commonsense advice. The book is filled with excellent and interesting real-life examples that further clarify and confirm the points that Ray makes with his *Run-Improve-Grow* model. So, go ahead! Be *fearless* and become a *liberated leader!* You, your employees, and all of your stakeholders will be better off for it, and you'll add meaningful value to your business."

—Duff Young, owner, Perspective Advisors, LLC

"Ray Attiyah has a deep technical understanding based on years of experience in business and innovation combined with a rare talent for communicating critical issues very simply. In *The Fearless Front Line*, Ray provides a fresh road map to empower front line staff. In turn, it infuses innovative change into your business. Simply put, this refreshing and inspiring perspective is a must read."

—Dora Anim, MPA, VP, Quality and Data,
Greater Cincinnati Health Council

THE FEARLESS
FRONT LINE

THE FEARLESS FRONT LINE

THE KEY TO LIBERATING LEADERS TO IMPROVE AND GROW THEIR BUSINESS

RAY ATTIYAH

bibliomotion
books + media

First published by Bibliomotion, Inc.

33 Manchester Road
Brookline, MA 02446
Tel: 617-934-2427
www.bibliomotion.com

Printed in the United States of America

Library of Congress Cataloging-in-Publication Data

Attiyah, Ray.
    The fearless front line : the key to liberating leaders to improve and grow the business / Ray Attiyah.
        pages cm
    ISBN 978-1-937134-61-7 (hardcover : alk. paper)—
ISBN 978-1-937134-62-4 (ebook)—ISBN 978-1-937134-63-1
(enhanced ebook)
    1. Leadership. 2. Corporate culture. 3. Organization.
4. Management. I. Title.
    HD57.7.A825 2013
    658.4'092—dc23
                        2012047162

*To my mom and dad, for showing me the satisfaction
of teaching, reminding me to be thankful for what we have
rather than what we don't, and for encouraging me to be fearless.*

*To my three daughters, who remind me every day the
importance of fostering environments that allow everyone to
fearlessly pursue their unique talents and curiosity.*

*To my wife, whose unconditional love and support have
encouraged me to pursue my passion.*

*To all teachers—at home, in schools, and in the workplace—who
really care and act fearlessly to support others' future success.*

Foreword

I had the pleasure of meeting Ray Attiyah about ten years ago. My boss was committed to making our company best in class, and he didn't want to look at our competitors as models—he wanted look outside our industry. So, one day he asked me to meet this guy, whom I first mistook for the next in a long line of tiresome, predictable consultants. What's more, most of the work done by Ray and his team was in manufacturing. Not only were we not a manufacturing company, we were an elite professional firm in the financial industry. "What could this guy ever offer me?" I thought to myself.

Surprisingly, what he offered weren't answers but questions. They were the types of questions that quickly gave insight into what was important to him. He asked first about our customers, then about my priorities, and finally about my front line. There was a deep connection in this man's mind between these factors, as well as their place within the entire system. It was a brief encounter with a man who would eventually change the way I thought about operations—a day I'll never forget.

That's because his questions weren't the kind that typical consultants ask—his questions took a direct and actionable slant. His first question to me was, "What do your customers pay for?" Not, "What do you do?" Not, "What does your organization do?" Ray and I went on to discuss the operations I had responsibility for. He was genuinely interested in not only what we did, but in how we did it. More importantly, he was interested in what systems we used to deliver *improved* results through our people each day. He was genuinely interested in our company's unique abilities and talents.

Ray was surprised to learn that we already had a set of concrete operational metrics and an actionable balanced scorecard that we used and monitored each day. Then his questions became more targeted and mission focused, and I really learned what made Ray different. "What are the problems that you are most struggling with?" "What do *you* spend your time on each day?" He proceeded to ask me about my direct reports—"Where were *they* spending *their* time?"

Our scorecard and current metrics couldn't answer those questions. Ray was intently focused on the behaviors of the organization, not just the numbers that everyone else looked at. He was probing at a level that was both rare and compelling, like a master teacher. Even though we had solid operational metrics, we were not fully leveraging the talent in our organization or the ideas they had every day. Ray wanted me to understand that while we were delivering excellent (and improving) operational results daily, we needed to engage in discussions and exercises that would allow us to achieve outstanding results and, at the same time, improve operational effectiveness dramatically beyond the measures we were reviewing.

At a critical point in our conversation, Ray asked me for a favor. He felt that the particular challenges facing my organization were different from previous challenges he had dealt with, and he wanted time to reflect and respond to these opportunities. We committed to getting back together in four to six weeks.

About a month later, I sat down with Ray over lunch. He suggested that perhaps the challenge my organization most needed to deal with was its success. What Ray said next has been stated many times and in countless books but never quite as pointedly or profoundly as when Ray said it to me.

He again asked where I spent my time—and why. He asked how a senior leader could most benefit his or her organization. Was it by being on the floor dealing with challenges? Or, might a leader better serve the company by working with peers in other organizations to look for broader organizational improvements? Perhaps, he suggested, there were growth opportunities being missed. Ray asked me where my middle managers spent their time. I had previously told him that in the event of a problem at the company, everyone showed up to engage in the problem-solving process. While that may sound like terrific teamwork—and it was—it also illustrated that we had opportunities to improve how we worked together, and how we solved problems. Eureka! We were spending too much time managing every single problem and not enough time looking at the bigger picture.

Ray grabbed a napkin and sketched a simple pyramid. He labeled three sections from bottom to top—Run, Improve, Grow. The explanation of Run-Improve-Grow was simple. Our front lines were responsible and accountable for getting the work done each day. Our middle management was responsible and accountable for driving dramatic and sustainable improvement throughout the organization. Our senior management was responsible for delivering bold, new opportunities to grow and transform the work we did.

This example no doubt sounds elementary, and yet how common it is for our organizations to stray from that simplicity and become overcomplicated! That simple lunch meeting began to change and enhance everything I practiced as a leader. With Ray's sage words in mind, I set to work simplifying my company. With purpose, I began to liberate my front line, and in so doing I liberated myself. The results were shockingly immediate.

The front line began to move to where the work was rather than wait on work to come to it. Within thirty days, the engagement of the entire team had skyrocketed—people felt they had the tools to be successful and saw their ideas being implemented. I had a better understanding of our business—where we excelled and where we faced challenges—and began working on issues that had previously been perceived as outside our control.

Within a very short time, our team won a prestigious teamwork award typically reserved for manufacturing companies, but even better was the fact that Gallup survey scores showed that our employees were more engaged, they felt they were making a more significant impact, and they felt trusted.

There's no way any of that would have been remotely possible if Ray hadn't shared with me how it is that leaders become successful—a lesson that has resulted in both my professional and personal growth. Each level of management has a role to play, and when those roles are played effectively, good things keep happening. Effective growth leads to improved outcomes, and improved outcomes lead to opportunities for growth. It's a virtuous cycle. But how do we encourage each leader to stretch beyond his or her past successes? How do we open up avenues of growth for all of our leaders? Run, Improve, Grow.

If you're planning on jumping around from page to page searching for incremental improvement ideas, *The Fearless Front Line* is probably not the book for you. But, if you're looking for a full-fledged transformation guidebook and want a master teacher for the guide, you've found the right book. Ray's principles are fairly fundamental, but they're presented in a methodical way that actually inspires people to action. And it's a replicable process that can be communicated and adopted throughout your entire organization.

I'm not going to sugar-coat it: transformation takes effort and risk. It requires trying things that are uncomfortable. But it will also create excitement in the front lines and sustainable improvement across your balanced scorecard. And if a guy like me from an elite company in what's considered a pretty stodgy industry can do it, so can you. I hope you will have the courage to try something new, get uncomfortable, and embrace great success— it's the only outcome from using Ray's method.

Mike Bull,
SVP Customer Transaction Services
at a world-renowned financial services firm

Contents

Foreword   ix

Introduction: The Fearless Organization: Consider
the Possible   xv

PART I
RUN: Creating a Fearless Front Line

1 Meet the Marathon Manager: Running
All the Time   3

2 Develop a Fearless Culture: "I Run This Place"   23

3 Empower the Front Line to Lead: Move Over,
Management   37

PART II
IMPROVE: Liberating Leaders to
Do Their Best Work

4 Transfer the Winning Momentum: Ignite
the Spark   61

5 Upgrade Management Systems: A Liberated
Manager Emerges   81

6 Fuel Proactive Improvements: A Play-to-Win
Culture Emerges   107

PART III
GROW: Blazing a Trail for Growth

7 Make (Then Keep) Bold Promises: Confidence
in Flawless Execution   131

8 Place (and Win) Bold Bets: Fail Fast,
Then Go Big   155

9 Scout (Then Place) Talent: Building
Your Grow Team   177

Endnotes   197
Acknowledgments   199
Index   203

The Fearless Organization: Consider the Possible

Much of our time is spent working—some forty, sixty, even eighty hours per week. That's more time awake than we spend with our friends or family and rivals the time we spend sleeping. Work is such a significant part of our lives that it even affects the quality of our sleep. Shouldn't the time we spend at work be worth it? Shouldn't that time be filled with a sense of purpose and accomplishment and not just packed with appointments and never-ending task lists? Shouldn't we be energized by the efforts and successes of our work team rather than drained by them? Shouldn't work be a time to learn, a time to engage with others to do something great, a time to be with people who enjoy what they are doing? And shouldn't the energizing effects of our work cascade over into our personal lives so our family and friends can see and feel our positive energy every day, instead of seeing us perpetually distracted with a phone to our ear?

Most, if not all, of us wouldn't hesitate to answer those questions with a resounding "YES!" That's because, deep down, we believe work should be more than just getting through a daily task list, checking off items as we finish them. Work should be a place that builds energy, not drains it. Work should provide opportunities for growth and improvement that bring out the best in us as individuals, as teams, and as entire organizations. Work should be such a positive force in our daily lives that those around us can't help but notice and be affected by our energy.

Too often, however, work isn't like that at all. Instead of energizing us, it traps us. Instead of inspiring us, it dulls our senses. The workplace is full of bureaucracy and negative complexity. Layer upon layer of systems and processes intended to keep everything running smoothly derail us on a daily basis. (Sometimes key people don't even know why these processes exist.) What's worse, instead of simplifying processes to solve the problems, our organizations keep adding more systems to the tangle already in place. We end up spending more time making sure to dot our i's and cross our t's than we do creating inspiring and innovative "new" work. Work feels like an old city with nothing but blind alleys or narrow, congested, one-way streets. We can't seem to get where we want to go, at least not quickly and without a significant extra effort. Indeed, after routinely spending that effort for little result, cynicism and mediocrity set in. We are trapped.

In an environment like that, nearly everyone in the company is toiling with the same goal: keep the systems and processes in check and get the product—any product—out the door. The systems and processes themselves often seem like the primary focus of the organization. Unnecessarily complex systems have an intense gravitational pull. Commonly, everyone in the organization is working in some capacity to keep the systems from spiraling out of control, even if it means adding more processes and procedures to keep everything in line. The sad part is that, without even realizing it, we ourselves become complicit in adding to the complexity that traps us.

Not all companies are like that. Some shine like beacons of excellence and growth in the crowded market. Think for a moment. You can probably name several, small and large, in your neighborhood, in your country, and in the world. There's seemingly no end to what these companies can do, create, and deliver. They seem to make a game of topping themselves! Their growth and excellence appear to know no bounds. So what's the difference? What makes the difference between true growth and a stifling existence? What's the difference between those companies that shine and the ones where work is a slog, apathy is everywhere, and products and people are mediocre at best? And how can your organization become a company that makes work a joy and excellence and innovation a mission?

The key is in liberating leaders. In companies where complicated systems reign, nearly everyone has his hands in the daily details of producing the product or delivering the services. Managers *and* frontline employees (and top executives and sometimes even the CEO) are tangled up in running the day-to-day aspects of the business, or the Run. The frontline activities are so unpredictable, unreliable, and complicated, and the systems surrounding them are so often superfluous, that managers can't seem to pull themselves away. (As you can imagine, this situation frustrates managers and employees alike.) Time and energy are consumed by urgent but unimportant tasks rather than activities that produce sustained personal and organizational growth. Managers have difficulty forgetting bad situations, and that inability to let go shakes their confidence in their frontline team and its activities. To compensate for their lack of confidence in the Run, managers become conditioned to overmanage and underlead. Regaining confidence is an uphill fight. So, while managers are stuck in the front line, they're not leading or pursuing activities that propel growth and innovation.

The precondition for liberating managers is having a front line that can operate reliably, excellently, and independently day in and day out every day of every week of every year. The Run needs to be rock solid—perpetually. It's the foundation of the entire organization. Yet, at the same time that the Run needs to be solid, it can't be rigid. It also needs to evolve and transform as the company innovates and grows. A Run like that involves getting the entire company, and particularly the front line, to be fearless. The front line needs to feel powerful, not powerless. It needs to be freed from worrying about senseless initiatives, ridiculous mandates, and unnecessary meetings and e-mails. It needs to be trusted, encouraged, and accountable to itself. It needs to be emboldened.

Run-Improve-Grow can get you and your organization to fearless. It can show you how to embrace bold. By implementing Run-Improve-Grow, organizations finally arrive at consistent excellent performance, free of the dramatic ups and downs that often take place when external changes require new plans or procedures. The first part of this book, Run, describes how to use the principles of Run-Improve-Grow to build a solid—and simplified—foundation that focuses on excellence and empowers the front line to be fearless and take true ownership of essential day-to-day operations.

The second part, Improve, explains how to capitalize on the momentum created by the fearless front line to liberate the organization's managers. Management systems, leadership styles, and the entire mind-set of the organization are all transformed in the Improve. With a fearless front line, simplified management system, and new organizational attitude, an organization is ready to launch boldly into the Grow. The third part of the book, then, outlines what the organization needs to do to make (then keep) bold promises, place (then win) bold bets, and scout (then hire) bold people. Senior managers have been freed to pursue strategic innovations and new opportunities that will propel the company to greater relevancy, ever-higher levels of excellence, and profitable growth.

It doesn't stop there, however. Run-Improve-Grow isn't confined to a beginning, middle, and end. Run-Improve-Grow is a perpetual model that approaches improvement as a continuously moving system that stimulates a culture of consistent relevancy, new growth, and constant innovation. For that reason, Run-Improve-Grow has near-universal applicability. It's not geared for a particular type of organization in a particular set of circumstances. The principles work for *any* organization—no matter how unique you think your situation is or how specialized and different your industry is. Run-Improve-Grow is based on fundamental principles that are universally true for every system and collection of people. So, even though many of the examples presented in this book relate to operations and manufacturing, Run-Improve-Grow has been applied in many organizations, functions, and industries. Whether a leader is struggling to guide an organization to stay afloat or create a bolder vision for an already flourishing team, Run-Improve-Grow has helped create and establish a culture of sustained success and innovation.

That's because Run-Improve-Grow is a holistic, well-proven system that integrates technical improvement tools, humanistic leadership practices, professional business standards, and a visionary entrepreneurial orientation. Run-Improve-Grow allows organizations to (re)create themselves over and over and over again, each time achieving newer, more deeply satisfying levels of growth.

Imagine what it would feel like if your organization had:

- confident frontline leaders and employees able to handle the complexity that comes with true (new) growth;
- efficient systems and processes owned by the people most closely connected to them;
- a continuous-improvement mind-set that permeates the organization's culture;
- a unified vision of peak performance in which your top performers are driven to even higher levels;
- time for mid-level leaders to focus on proactive improvements and for top-level leaders to focus on growth-related activities;
- open systems of communication; and
- more productive frontline employees who hold themselves accountable, have ownership of their own solutions, and have a better understanding of the entire business.

And what if you could reliably:

- grow confidently in the direction of your choosing?
- promise the moon—and deliver it regularly?

- provide the most innovative solutions to your customers' problems?
- attract the industry's best talent?
- command premium pricing of products and services that are heavily in demand and are far superior to any alternatives?
- enjoy working every day?
- experience no compromises—can you grow, simplify, *and* attract and engage the best talent?

Imagine a workplace that is free from the stress of managers and staff always finding problems but rarely acting on solutions, a workplace where teams establish and agree on clear standards of excellence, and a workplace where people are encouraged to propose bold ideas and then make them realities? Run-Improve-Grow makes that workplace possible.

The ultimate payoff is the virtuous circle. Excellence at anything—sports, music, art, cooking, business—requires practice. When you start something new, like playing the piano, the practice is arduous. Your fingers feel heavy and slow. They plod along, stumbling over the keys. Your eyes can't decide if they should be watching your hands or reading the music, so you're constantly losing your place. The notes aren't marked on the piano keys, and the score is in a completely different language. Half an hour of practice feels like a month. You might get discouraged and stop. The more you practice, and the more you focus on your practice, however, the better you become. Your eyes don't have to look at your hands anymore and can decode many notes on the score simultaneously. Your fingers get used to the movements and find the right keys more quickly. When you strike a wrong note, you keep going (rather than stopping to bang the keys in frustration). Soon, what you're playing sounds like music, and you want to perfect more, and more difficult, songs. You experience joy through the music *and* through your ability to produce it.

The same basic concept applies to playing par golf, baking a cake, drawing blood, sewing a dress, designing a software package, designing a fixture, running an experiment, or packing a skid. It applies to hobbies and to work. It applies in the emergency room, front office, back office, production line, storefront, warehouse, and the research and development department. The more you do something, the better you get; the better you get, the more enjoyable the activity is.

The same is true of the improvement and transformation process. Run-Improve-Grow is built on the principle that practice in a perpetual process can create meaningful, sustainable growth, and the approach has been proven many times over with many success stories across industries. Today's business environment is nothing if not fluid. Companies—and their employees—need to adapt continuously, and arguably they need to adapt more quickly and more regularly than ever before. Forget the bluster. In a fast-paced, ever-changing environment, you need reliable, dependable backup for people making bolder and bolder moves. You need people throughout the organization who are fearless.

That's why becoming practiced in the improvement and transformation process is so crucial. If you keep reacting reflexively to the changing environment by rolling out the latest and greatest continuous-improvement programs, you'll always be running in all directions with no destination. Your fate and the fate of your organization will be dependent on (or hostage to) externalities.

I advocate a simpler, more purposeful approach. This book will help you create a bold road map. As you read, think big and start small. Stop being buffeted by the churning rapids of the business environment. Strap on a helmet, grab an oar, and fearlessly direct your own course.

Keep it simple and be fearless.

Ray

PART I

RUN

CREATING A FEARLESS
FRONT LINE

1

Meet the Marathon Manager: Running All the Time

Business is active. With the exception of occasional slow periods, which are characteristic of economic cycles, business comes as close to creating a perpetual motion machine as anything else out there. Business is busy and complex.

Complexity is many moving parts working toward an objective with a high degree of difficulty. I don't think I have to tell you that running a business is difficult *because* it requires so many moving parts. Business is inherently complex, but all too often we make running a business more complex than it needs to be. Too many people involved in too many processes. It only takes one or two moving parts falling out of synchronization to cause systems and processes to become unreliable. Over time, the inherent complexity that comes with running a business seems too difficult to overcome. How do we let that happen?

Our goal is to return business to its simplest state by removing negative complexity. To do that, we first need to look at how we got here in the first place.

Where Are You Spending *Your* Time?

Where do you spend your time?

When I asked an operations manager named Mike Bull that exact question, he told me he tried to spend as much time possible with his customers developing new programs. That's a rather uncommon answer, but his company was in the process of making systematic changes to improve customer service. But even as he was spending time with his customers trying to find solutions to service and delivery issues, his group was suffering from inconsistency. One week they'd hit a record level of performance, and then the week after they'd have some challenges with turnaround times to customers.

His company was experiencing the classic "sawtooth effect." A company aims to raise its performance standards, but it has a difficult time hitting those new standards consistently, so managers get dragged back into the daily operations to eliminate inconsistencies. And while managers are trying to bring up the bottom performers, the top performers become frustrated with losing and their performance returns to the old standard. Then everyone—managers and operators—has to start over from square one.

Sawtooth Effect

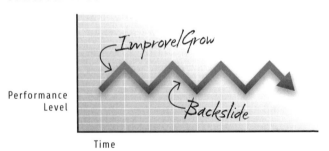

Performance
Level

Time

Figure 1.1

Mike was working hard to create a higher standard of excellence within his organization, and his employees seemed to get that. But when he recounted all he was doing, he kept saying, "I am involved in...." I began to wonder why he was spending so much time in *all* of those activities.

Then it clicked: What if his frontline leaders had the confidence to take full ownership of the daily process-improvement activities so Mike could spend even more time developing new customer solutions? What new levels of performance and growth could his team achieve?

I met Mike for lunch and asked him my burning question: What if he could focus even more time on his customers? His answer was textbook. He'd be able to plan better, have more collaborative relationships with his customers, and, as a result, bring in more profitable work.

If he thought the company could bring in more work if he spent more time with his customers, why wasn't he doing *that* instead of all the other work he was involved in?

When I asked him, he said, "We need to make sure we are consistently performing before we can start working on new initiatives. I need to make sure we're delivering our promises on existing commitments before we promise anything new."

I pressed him. "Sure, but why does it have to be *you* who ensures your team performs consistently?"

He didn't reply. He just gave me a wry smile to show me he understood my point. I drew a pyramid on my lunch napkin, divided it horizontally into three sections, and explained the concept of Run-Improve-Grow.

Run-Improve-Grow

Figure 1.2

The Run

Figure 1.3

At the base of the triangle is the **Run**, or the day-to-day activities necessary to produce your products or deliver your service, which includes securing orders of existing products and services from customers in existing markets and in existing geographies. The Run is the assembly of a Ford truck. It is the cooking and delivery of a steak at Morton's. It is stitching a child's wound in the emergency room after a bike accident. The Run is the process of making and delivering a product or service that is used by a customer, client, or patient. When the Run can't function reliably and independently of management involvement, it strains resources by pulling managers away from their *most-value-added* functions.

This is where organizations fall into the sawtooth effect. Top-level managers launch growth initiatives, because without growth, organizations can't add people. But without people, leaders can't delegate responsibility. When leaders can't delegate, they're stuck in the Run, so they can't innovate. Without new and innovative ideas, products, and services, organizations can't grow. Without innovation and growth, organizations don't have capital to invest in the future, so managers don't attempt growth initiatives. And the cycle continues. So the ability to Improve and to Grow starts with a rock-solid, reliable Run.

Every organization (and, of course, its leaders) is susceptible to falling into a sawtooth effect, but in the past, only small businesses were at high risk of stagnating in the Run. Without a deep bench of talent, small businesses would try simultaneously to balance the increased complexity of new initiatives, higher customer expectations, and poor leverage for price increases.

Today, businesses of all sizes are susceptible because of reduced staffing, greater demand, and higher complexity. For example, small businesses tend to stay small because they're unable to transition from the Run to the Grow. In a small business's infancy, growth may come opportunistically, but over time, the company can stress as it swallows new work because the owners or entrepreneurs are the ones running everything. Every business starts with hard work from the owner, but for the business to get out of that newborn phase, the owner and key players need to disengage from the daily Run. By setting up confident systems in the daily Run, leaders can focus on more strategic and valuable aspects of the business.

Having a solidified Run led by an organization's front line is crucial to Run-Improve-Grow sustainability. Most mid-level and top leaders spend time in the Run out of necessity because they are doing whatever it takes to get product out the door. Without a solidified Run led by the front line, managers get dragged down in the Run, preventing them from working in areas where they can add the most value to their organization and its customers—in the Improve and Grow functions.

How much time should leaders at various levels in the organization spend in the Run versus the Improve and the Grow? The answer may surprise you. Let's take a look at the ideal time allocation in Run-Improve-Grow.

World Class Time Allocation

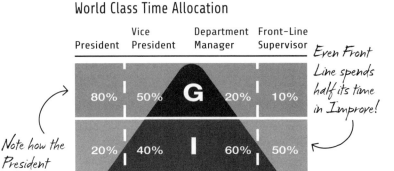

Figure 1.4

Most likely, however, your organization's time allocation looks nothing like that. If you work in a large business, the time allocation of the various people in your organization probably looks more like this:

Actual Time Allocation in Large Businesses

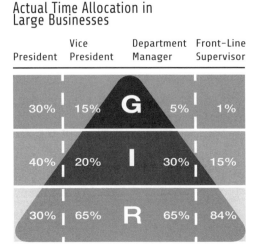

Figure 1.5

If you work in a small business, you might think the above allocation of time is ridiculously optimistic and overly weighted to the Grow. You're right. The time allocation of the various people in your smaller organization probably looks more like this:

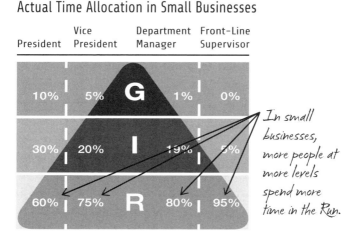

Actual Time Allocation in Small Businesses

President	Vice President	Department Manager	Front-Line Supervisor
10%	5%	**G** 1%	0%
30%	20%	**I** 19%	5%
60%	75%	**R** 80%	95%

In small businesses, more people at more levels spend more time in the Run.

Figure 1.6

What a difference between the real and the ideal! Whether you're at a small or large company, the majority of dynamic action in your organization is taking place at the bottom of the RIG triangle, in the Run—which is completely opposite of where dynamic action should be taking place.

Because the Run is comprised of the day-to-day operations that sustain an organization's existence, the activities of the Run directly and indirectly create the value proposition the organization offers to the customer today. Run activities also affect the immediate revenue and earnings potential of the company. Everything a company offers today hinges on the Run.

Because of that, you might think that a culture focused on the Run makes a business successful. A Run-centric culture shows operational commitment to the customer at all levels, right?

Wrong. A Run-centric culture is actually the opposite of what a business needs to be successful. The adage about too many cooks spoiling the soup is as true in business as it is in the kitchen. There are reasons that the RIG model diagram shows clear delineations for the Run, the Improve, and the Grow. The Run is not something everyone in the company should be involved in. (Even if you don't agree with me now, by the end of this stage, I'm confident you'll change your mind.) So why can't you stop running?

How Do Run-Centric Cultures Develop?

No one shows up to work in the morning with the intent to perform poorly. Most people want to be productive and to contribute. A keen desire to be involved and to influence perfection can pull people to engage in the Run even when it's not their job.

More often, however, a Run-centric culture evolves without much thought or effort. In fact, it is a lack of thought that can foster a Run-centric culture in which too many people who shouldn't be are involved in the Run. That is, too many managers are fully engaged in the Run rather than in the Improve or the Grow. You might even say they're meddling.

What keeps managers feeling responsible for the Run? Why can't they let go and leave the Run to the frontline leaders? Negative personal beliefs and unreliable systems and processes.

Negative Personal Beliefs

Three main negative personal beliefs make up the rotten core of a Run-centric culture: lack of confidence, lack of trust, and assuming negative intent. These beliefs get passed from managers to frontline employees, from frontline employees to managers, and back and forth among frontline employees themselves.

Managers who hover over daily details to scrutinize or institutionalize the Run cause frontline employees and leaders to wonder, "Why spend time doing something if someone else is going to change it or do it over anyway?" Think of it this way: an average employee who knows his work is going to be rejected, redone, or replicated by the boss has little incentive to do his best work.

When employees see the boss give an employee or group of employees a no-confidence vote, peers eventually begin to lack confidence in one another. When leaders don't have confidence in their front line, and when the frontline employees don't have confidence in their coworkers and the processes they use, work becomes chaotic, disorganized, and slow.

Lack of confidence breeds lack of trust. Whereas confidence is a belief in what an individual or department says *can* be done, trust is a belief in what an individual or department says *will* be done. If you tell a client that you *can* build a house in five months but it takes six months to complete, confidence might be shaken but not destroyed. But if you tell the client that you *will* have the house completed in five months and it isn't, the bond of trust has been broken and the implications are significant. The client will think twice before trusting you again.

If you don't trust a frontline employee to get a job done and done right, you're going to find a way to work around her. You may even do the job yourself, in whole or in part, to make sure that what you have told your customers *will* get done *does* get done. That work-around will confirm your personal belief that nothing can get done without your involvement, and voilà, you're smack in the middle of the Run.

Lack of trust is also an issue with frontline employees at the peer-to-peer level, particularly when collaboration is part of the job. If one member of your team is unreliable and produces work of inconsistent—or consistently poor—quality or perpetually delivers work late, the other team members are not going to trust delegating responsibilities to him. In that way, top performers take on more and more responsibilities, and their actual job responsibilities (the ones they were hired to do) become lost in the mix. Without trust, people spend more time talking about the problems than solving them.

To gain trust, frontline employees and managers must develop relationships. That means employees and managers need to be engaged with one another. There needs to be enough interaction that all parties have experiences upon which they can build their relationships. For a Run-Improve-Grow implementation to work, relationships need to be based on goodwill and good intent. Both parties in a relationship need to assume good intent and mutual respect.

Jumping to negative conclusions about people's actions only perpetuates negative relationships. When we give people the benefit of the doubt and assume good intent behind their actions, we encourage positive relationships. In companies fraught with defensiveness and distrust, relationships can be tainted with condescension and an undercurrent of blame. If the customer changes his mind, he's inconveniencing the employee. If the vendor points out a problem with an order, the employee perceives a personal attack and becomes defensive. If managers want employees to do a time-management study, employees think they're being monitored unfairly because their bosses don't like or trust them.

Managers and employees need to know how to engage in the conversation without taking everything personally. Building positive relationships takes patience and commitment on all sides. When two employees, supervisors, or managers can discuss their displeasure without involving their bosses, that's success. Communication that is simple, direct, timely, objective, and fact based is the most effective.

Unreliable Systems and Processes

Run-centric cultures aren't just a product of poor communication and bad relationships. Unreliable systems and processes play a significant role as well. Let's face it, reliability is boring. Turn on the faucet and water comes out, not fireworks. But every time you turn on the faucet, water still flows. We've become so confident in and trusting of our local water departments, we don't just expect water to flow. We *know* it will. We rely on it.

But what if water didn't come out the next time you opened the faucet? You would wonder what was wrong. Then what? You'd try it again. And again. By the third time, you wouldn't trust that the water company was going to deliver what you had come to assume it would. You'd buy and store crates of bottled water; you'd come up with provisions to catch rainwater; you'd conserve. All those extra behaviors and systems would be created for the sole purpose of managing your water usage because you couldn't depend on the water company. Extra systems and processes like those provide a safety net for unpredictable outages and failures in service. The extra plans and procedures help us manage "what if" scenarios.

Just as we create work-arounds in our personal lives, we create superfluous processes in our organizations to provide a safety net for system failures. The more mature the company, the more intricate and embedded the contingency work-arounds tend to be. That's negative complexity.

Start-up businesses begin with the most basic systems necessary to serve their customers. But over time and as businesses mature, experiences and negative complexity add clutter to p

rocesses and procedures, often without management noticing. Think of the daily provisions that we add because we lack confidence and trust in flawless Run execution:

- Extra meetings
- Check-up e-mails
- Uneccessary conference calls
- Detailed reports
- Useless measurements and data collection
- Audits
- E-mail distribution lists
- Repeated e-mail chains
- Emergency phone calls
- Sign-off requirements
- Approval restrictions
- Additional systems, procedures, and processes

Clutter is a compromise; it's a response to the unreliable nature of our frontline Run. When the Run doesn't operate consistently at peak performance, we compensate by adding layers of systems and processes. Look again at the list of extras that get layered into the Run. They all serve to keep organizational attention focused on the Run. All that clutter, however, is nothing more than hurdles and obstacles for the front line."

In addition to junking up the Run, superfluous systems also prevent team development. Instead of a group of individuals working together with flexibility and unity, workers come together around negative norms (complaining, exasperation, fatigue). The systemic clutter sends a message that management thinks the front line is incapable of handling the Run without support or special help.

After a while, all that clutter becomes institutionalized, particularly if the results it produces are considered successful. As the level of useless activity increases, employees and managers alike become oblivious to the fact that what's now taken as gospel started as a way to compensate for some deficiency.

At one company, the work-around taken as gospel was actually nicknamed "the bible," a spreadsheet that tracked all of the plant's urgent (late) orders. In actuality, the bible wasn't working: the organization's on-time delivery was a dreadful 30 percent. When the bible was first instituted, the the plant manager could maintain it. Then, as the volume and complexity of work increased, he couldn't keep up.

The bible may have seemed like a novel way to take control of the perceived scheduling problem, but in reality, it was a work-around. The work had become more complex, and instead of redesigning the scheduling methodology to meet new and greater demands, managers created "the bible" as an expediting tool. Managers (and frontline employees) frequently mistake extra processes like scheduling bibles for being the Run. The entire organization is so myopically focused on what it *thinks* is the Run that it neglects the *actual* Run. Running around is not the Run. Remember that the Run consists of the day-to-day operations of the organization that sustain the organization's existence. Needless meetings, extra e-mails, and layered processes do not sustain an organization's existence. But paradoxically, the focus on the embellished Run is what makes a Run-centric culture.

Who serves as the life raft that helps frontline employees pass through the bog? The institutionalized manager. When managers enable this Run-centric culture through their involvement in the daily operations, the managers themselves become part of the dysfunctional Run system—they become institutionalized. Institutionalized managers are constantly Running—I like to call them marathon managers. Marathon managers who don't change their frontline systems end up becoming part of the frontline system itself. Work gets done through them.

As marathon managers become firmly embedded in the Run, a vacuum intensifies in the Improve. The company now lacks the right level of focus on the Improve, and that inattention either prevents the Grow or creates chaos and lower profitability when the Grow comes. The Run is, in effect, disconnected from the Grow and, therefore, from long-term organizational relevance.

Do you know any marathon managers? Are there any in your organization? Are *you* a marathon manager?

What Pulls Mid-Level Managers into the Run?

In the Run-Improve-Grow system, the role of the mid-level manager is to work the Improve. That middle level connects the Run to the Grow in a substantive way, and without that connection, the Run is unable to evolve to meet the organization's future growth potential. It's critical to understand what pulls mid-level managers into the Run so you can learn what can free them from it.

In working with companies of different sizes in a variety of industries, I've noticed three conditions that create situations whereby mid-level managers get drawn into the Run. The first is the manager who holds a personal belief that nothing can get done without her involvement. This manager lives a self-fulfilling prophecy. The dysfunctional Run is so chaotic that the manager finds herself dashing from emergency to emergency. This manager does nothing to wean her subordinates off her involvement. After being the linchpin in this kind of environment for a period of time, the manager becomes so connected to the Run that she can't imagine what her job would be if it didn't involve Running.

Other managers are trapped in the Run because they enjoy it. Managers who enjoy being involved in the Run may like the frenetic activity characteristic of the dysfunctional Run, or they prefer the immediacy and short-term focus the dysfunctional Run demands. Sometimes marathon managers truly enjoy frontline activities more than Improve activities. These managers feel more confident executing than designing. But by continuing to execute day-to-day responsibilities, these managers insert themselves into functions that don't maximize their value to the organization.

"There's a level of comfort in everybody," a mid-level leader once told me when I asked about his team's comfort zones. "Even me. I remember a time when I told [an associate] that I was becoming a really good change agent. Apparently, he disagreed. Before I got into work the next day, he moved my desk from one side of the room to the other, knowing I would flip out. And I did. He showed me that if I couldn't receive a change as simple as moving my desk a couple of feet, then I wasn't as much of a change agent as I had believed."

As we continued talking, he shared one final piece of advice that I want to share with you: "In life, it's the people who do drills or training that stay sharp and nimble. In business, we don't run many drills. So unless you prepare people for change, they'll be resistant to accept it, kind of like I was with my desk."

When managers stay in their comfort zones, they are playing not to lose. Leaders need to create environments where managers feel uncomfortable when they play not to lose. These managers need to be pushed out of their comfort zones. To create new standards for mid-tier leaders, top leaders have to set new expectations of behavior for mid-tier leaders as part of an upgraded management system (a subject we'll cover in greater depth in chapter 6). Left to their own devices, managers who enjoy the Run will always revert to the Run unless leaders set—and follow through on—new expectations.

The final condition that pulls managers into the Run is the fear of not having all the answers. The longer a marathon manager is embedded in the Run, the more likely it is he feels pressure to have an answer for everything. Subordinates look to the marathon manager to fix everything. The fear of not having a ready answer may even cause the manager to offer *any* answer to maintain his "answer man" status. That answer may not be the *best* answer, but it's *an* answer. Quick answers are rarely thought out or subjected to rigorous probing. And quick directives and answers accepted without scrutiny are often the original source of superfluous processes and systems that add a new and different layer of complexity and clutter.

Marathon managers:

- think nothing can get done without them;
- enjoy being involved in the Run;
- play not to lose; and
- are afraid of not having the answers.

How Do Frontline Employees Perceive Marathon Managers?

So far, I've mostly been describing the situation of a marathon manager from a manager's perspective, but it's also important to examine that situation from the employee's perspective. How do frontline employees perceive marathon managers who embed themselves in the Run? I've had conversations with thousands of frontline employees, and most often they perceive their marathon managers in one of two ways: authoritarian (the traffic cop) or stretched beyond capacity (the lonely wedge).

Authoritarian (The Traffic Cop)

An authoritarian marathon manager often embodies two of the three conditions that cause managers to become embedded in the Run: he is an answer man who believes that peak performance can't be achieved without his involvement. Therefore, he acts as a gatekeeper between frontline employees and organizational top leaders. Either no information gets from the front line to the back office (or vice versa), or the information that does pass through is fraught with miscommunication colored by the authoritarian manager's personal biases and beliefs. The authoritarian version of the marathon manager is a stifling presence because of his need to have everything under control (especially under *his* control). These managers concentrate power in themselves and favor blind submission over thoughtful discussion. There is no room for other views, opinions, questions, ideas, or alternative methods under the direction of these managers. Nothing happens in the Run without their direct involvement and approval.

Think of this manager as a traffic cop at an intersection that actually has a traffic signal or stop sign. Does having a traffic cop at a busy intersection—instead of a functioning and well-timed traffic light—really speed up the flow of traffic? More likely, traffic slows and drivers wonder what's taking so long. Until they get to the intersection, that is.

Like the traffic cop at the intersection, traffic cop marathon managers micromanage the daily Run, hovering to ensure every minute detail adheres to their directives. Over time, frontline employees come to expect micromanagement, so they naturally wait for the marathon manager to sign off on any and every daily activity. This frontline dependence halts progress. Ultimately, the Run becomes like that busy rush hour intersection where the marathon manager serves as the traffic cop.

Traffic cop marathon managers can be:

- bossy;
- know-it-alls;
- control freaks;
- explosive;
- micromanagers; and
- closed-minded.

The traffic cop marathon manager's mantra is "No" or "I didn't say you could do that."

Stretched Beyond Capacity (The Lonely Wedge)

The other category of marathon managers consists of those who are stretched beyond capacity, the lonely wedge. Similar to an authoritarian marathon manager, a lonely wedge gets stuck fire-fighting in the Run because she doesn't have support to clean up the fires that come as a result of unreliable systems and processes.

For those of you familiar with golf, the concept of the lonely wedge might be clear. If, however, you do not play golf, you need to know that golf clubs can be loosely divided into three categories: the woods (including the driver, or 1-wood), irons (including the pitching wedge), and the putter. Each club plays a very different role on the golf course. Players use the driver to get the ball off the tee and onto the fairway and the putter to get the ball in the hole once it's on the green. The irons, including the pitching wedge, work the space in between.

Drivers and putters are flashy and innovative, with new designs and technologies coming out yearly, but the pitching wedge is so forgettable that it's often actually left behind on the previous hole. The wedge chips the ball out of the woods or lifts it out of the sand after an errant drive to stage the ball on the green for the putter. How successful the wedge shot is determines how hard the putter has to work. The wedge, therefore, plays a critical, if thankless, role in any golf game.

In many organizations, frontline leaders stretched beyond their capacity often feel like a lonely wedge. They must be versatile enough to handle variability in demand, changing business models, poor execution by others, and last-minute (and often unreasonable) customer requirements. Often, the only form of acknowledgement they receive for the crucial role they play in the organization and its success is a larger workload with ever-increasing demands and expectations.

A lonely wedge is mentally prepared to put out fires, but she doesn't particularly know where they'll erupt. She manages in a state of perpetual hypervigilance, always anticipating the worst and worn out from tense expectation. Because she spends so much time waiting for problems to surface, she's perpetually distracted, and because so many problems *do* surface, she's massively time constrained. As a result of inadequate support and chronically expecting the worst ("What's *next*?!"), lonely wedge marathon managers are often tired, lethargic, and unfocused—not the best traits for an individual expected to inspire change!

Lonely wedge marathon managers can be:

- distracted;
- time constrained;
- searching;
- exhausted;
- exasperated;
- discouraged;
- indifferent;
- forgotten; and
- unfocused.

The mantra of the lonely wedge marathon manager is "What *now*?!"

How Do Marathon Managers Impact Your Organization?

Whether the mid-level managers in an organization are traffic cops or lonely wedges, constant involvement in the Run (in other words, marathon management) has a negative impact on the managers themselves, the frontline employees, and the organization as a whole.

Burnout is a major risk to running and firefighting constantly—marathon managers Run so intently that it may eventually consume all their energy. It takes a lot of effort to control everything in their environments! For an authoritarian, burnout is aggravated by an attitude of arrogance and contempt. For the lonely wedge, a sense of helplessness leads to physical and emotional burnout. Fatigue, depression, and anxiety color the relationships lonely wedge managers have with frontline employees.

Working for a depressed, exhausted, angry boss can be a nightmare, as his mood affects yours. It's not surprising that marathon managers have an impact beyond themselves.

In my experience, roughly 80 percent of an organization's workers are frontline employees, and 5 percent are frontline leaders (those traffic cops and lonely wedges).[1] That means 80 percent of the workforce learns about an organization's culture, behaviors, and vision from their frontline leaders. To frontline workers, a frontline leader is truly the face of an organization—the face that can either support or prevent the front line's effectiveness.

If frontline leaders have such a significant role in shaping the attitudes and behaviors of the frontline workers, then you can imagine what happens when that frontline leader is a marathon manager. (Maybe you don't need to imagine; maybe you already know firsthand.) The negative feelings of the marathon manger can't help but spill over into the front line.

Marathon managers also create dependence on the part of their subordinates. Because these managers are do-everything, know-everything, fix-everything types of people, they leave no space for their employees to become capable and independent workers. The implications of that kind of dependence for the organization are serious. The pool of capable people becomes shallower and shallower. The organization might as well be staffed entirely by new and entry-level employees who know little about the work.

By now, you're probably starting to feel the crushing negative implications of having marathon managers in your organization. Keeping frontline employees dependent on their managers is a guaranteed way to create chronic complacency. Employees don't feel they are able to contribute to the organization, so they become mentally distant from the work. Indeed, allowing marathon management to go unchecked results in managers and employees having only one thing in common: a cynical attitude toward work.

Shared cynicism fuels a **cynical cycle**, a self-perpetuating negativity loop bred from bad experiences and negative personal beliefs. Once employees at any level begin to participate in the cycle, a sustainable frontline-led Run is in jeopardy. Cynical cycles may start with individuals or even departments, but they can easily overwhelm an entire organizational culture like a contagious virus.

In cynical cultures, blame, condescension, and ill will are pervasive. The organization's character becomes marred by a culture of excuses. You can almost hear "*They* did this" and "But *they* did that" being volleyed back and forth. The us-versus-them mentality takes root and devastates curiosity as well as transparent communication. But most critically, the cynical cycle creates a fearful culture that is focused inward. Employees are so concerned about petty grievances, assigning blame, and jockeying for position that they become blind to the life force of the organization—its customers.

TAKEAWAYS

- A Run-centric culture is actually the opposite of what a business needs to be successful for the long haul.
- Cynical cycle perpetuates blame and undermines a fearless front line.
- Managers who hover over daily details to ensure the Run's completion implicitly give a no-confidence vote to their employees, and so frontline employees are no longer motivated to maximize their efforts.
- As businesses mature, they create clutter. Superfluous processes are added to create a safety net for unreliable systems, and the organization can't see clearly what it needs to do to be efficient and effective.
- Running around is not the Run.
- Marathon managers enable a dysfunctional Run.
- Marathon managers have serious and negative impact on themselves, on their subordinates, and on the organization as a whole.

Develop a Fearless Culture: "I Run This Place"

By now, I've painted a very unpleasant picture of a Run-centric culture and the marathon managers who sustain it. I've never met anyone who enjoyed working in or leading a cynical, Run-centric environment. So now the question is: What does it take to go from fearful to fearless?

Start by eliminating those same marathon managers who perpetuated a Run-centric cynical cycle. By that I don't mean fire them. You must eliminate the *need* for them.

How Can You Eliminate Marathon Managers?

The payoff for eliminating the need for marathon managers is significant. Examine figure 2.1. It's based on the workweek of a real marathon manager and assumes a forty-hour week as the baseline. Before the RIG implementation, he was spending 190 percent of his time in the Run. Combined with the 10 percent he spent on Improve, he was working eighty-hour weeks, necessitated by the fact that the company grew unexpectedly—and didn't have a solid Run system in place when it did. Notice how the allocation of his time shifted as the RIG implementation progressed and was sustained and improved over the next two years.

Time Allocation of an Actual Marathon Manager

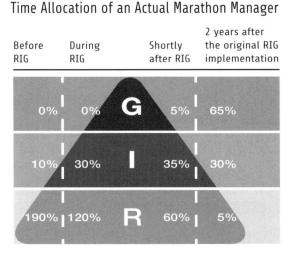

Before RIG	During RIG	Shortly after RIG	2 years after the original RIG implementation
0%	0%	5%	65%
10%	30%	35%	30%
190%	120%	60%	5%

Figure 2.1

Not only did this manager see his allocation shift very heavily from Run to Grow functions, he cut his workweek in half and decreased to a regular forty hours. Think of what that change means for him and for his organization!

Identify Most-Value-Added Functions

The ability to make such monumental shifts requires you to sort out the Run. The first step in that direction is identifying your employees' most-value-added functions. **Most-value-added (MVA) functions** are those functions that maximize an individual's highest and best use. Marathon managers may be able to add value by being involved in the Run, but it is not their highest and best use. In a five-star restaurant, the chef may be a very personable guy as well as a culinary genius, but that doesn't mean he should be the maître d' as well as the chef. His highest and best use is in the kitchen.

The concept of MVA and highest and best use is not exclusive to the Run. This critical concept applies throughout the organization. I once read an article about a CEO who would assemble every piece of furniture that his company ordered for its own use. When the company made a new hire, the CEO would even assemble the new employee's desk chair and set up the desk. Did the furniture need to be assembled by someone? Sure. But was that really the CEO's highest and best use? No. When *all* the employees in an organization are aligned with their MVA functions, the organization is ready to maximize the vertical and horizontal aspects of Run-Improve-Grow.

Most-value-added functions are not the same as value-added functions. Just because you're doing something that adds some value doesn't mean it's what you should be doing. Think about it. You might be a great fork truck driver but an even better setup man. You add value when you function as a fork truck driver, but you add more value when you function as a setup man. Your individual peak performance is as a setup man.

In Run-Improve-Grow, individuals reach peak performance when they execute their tasks flawlessly in a position where their strengths will add the most value; whether they are frontline employees or mid-tier leaders or top leaders, individuals can only achieve peak performance when their tasks are tailored to their strengths.

Flawless execution in an individual's most-value-added function (peak performance at the individual level) comes when each individual's strengths are understood and then matched to the right position in the company. Building relationships with frontline employees is the simplest way for leaders to identify the strengths of those employees. Once employee strengths are identified and agreed upon, leaders can align frontline employees with the jobs that need to be done. It's a simple process that, with thought and concern for others, simply takes purposeful effort.

Depending on how long you and your team have been with the organization, you may already have a sense of the areas each person has a passion for and excels in. You probably already know which employee you'd go to with a certain type of problem or to whom you'd assign a job of a certain level of difficulty.[1]

Once you have your frontline team assembled, with each member in the right position, you are poised to create a flawlessly executing Run without management involvement. We'll spend most of chapter 3 on this topic, so I won't go into detail here. What you need to take away at this point is that until the front line flawlessly executes the Run and is consistently delivering peak performance day after day after day, it will be impossible for the marathon manager to have the confidence and trust necessary for her to get out of the Run.

After your team is assembled, you're ready to get started making reactive improvements. Reactive improvements fix existing unreliable systems and processes that don't consistently deliver results at the current standard of performance. I can't stress this enough: an organization's leaders *must* articulate the standards of performance that relate to each of those desired system and process changes in order for them to be sustainable. Is 90 percent on-time delivery the standard, or is it 95 percent, or 99 percent? Is the expected quality a tolerance of .001 mm or .0001 mm or .00001 mm? Is the order turnaround time ten minutes, one hour, one week, two weeks, one month, or one year?

Whatever standards the organization's leaders believe will achieve their business objectives and meet their strategic plan, those standards need to be specified and shared throughout the organization. Broadcast them throughout the organization in such an obvious and regular manner that every employee knows them by heart. Make sure that no one can claim ignorance or forgetfulness. Everyone needs to be working toward a consistent and aligned level of performance through these reactive improvements.

Simplify the Run

Before the front line can really start flawlessly executing the Run in accordance with specified performance standards, the organization needs to clean up its processes and clear out the clutter that's clogging up its systems. And that's why the first order of business in a RIG implementation is identifying and making reactive improvements that simplify the Run.

With so many superfluous systems clouding the view of a defined performance standard, how can leaders identify and prioritize the systems and processes that need simplification? The first step involves starting with a clean sheet of paper and going down to the most fundamental level. Ask:

- What is the basic deliverable our customer wants?
- What does our customer do with our deliverable?
- How can we give that customer what they want in the fewest steps possible?

Imagine you are a one-person company and you have to do it all—take the orders, buy the materials, make the product or deliver the service, collect payment. You would probably figure out the fewest steps, or the purest process, to get all of that done. That's simplification. Companies with more than one employee find a way over time to add layers to that purest process. In RIG, you want to get back to that pure process. So identify those basic elements and then ask yourself why you're doing anything else—and when you started doing all those extras. This is an opportunity to understand how the organization has evolved. (You need to know how that evolution has occurred because later in the process you're going to need to justify why you're eliminating steps.)

At this point in RIG, expect a fight. People have an easier time adding crap than getting rid of it. If you don't believe me, tune in to an episode of the television show *Hoarders*. People on the show have accumulated so many belongings that they can barely move around in their homes. Viewers can see right away that the cherished belongings are just junk and clutter. But to the hoarders, they're absolutely essential parts of their identity. Getting hoarders to declutter is a grueling process. The deep clean that happens on *Hoarders* is similar to what companies need to do to simplify the Run. First, you have to clear out all the layers of systems and processes you've accumulated over time. Take your process to its purest state and try it. Identify breakdowns in delivering what's required and in the consistency of the process.

Those breakdown points are where you need to make reactive improvements. A word of caution, however: a breakdown point may not be the issue that ultimately needs to be improved. Just because an organization has a scheduling problem, for instance, doesn't necessarily mean scheduling is the issue that needs to be improved. For example, causes for not meeting the scheduling could include: materials from suppliers are chronically late; equipment breakdowns; or insufficient staffing. The customer may have changed the originally agreed-upon lead time. Different people may do their work differently, causing inconsistencies in the time it takes to complete the job. Rarely is there one cause for a problem, scheduling or otherwise; there are usually numerous root causes that compound the effects of the problem. Once you have a sense of the impact of each breakdown on your list, the next step is to begin finding root causes of the gap between where you are and the standard of performance you want to attain. In this step, practicing courage is critical. Be fearless. Sometimes people want to dance around root causes. Perhaps they don't want to give voice to complaints they have against coworkers. Perhaps they don't want to be perceived as negative or blaming. Other times, people are eager to start pointing fingers and calling out colleagues whose work they think is inadequate or of low quality. Leaders need to sift through all the contributions to see clearly what the root causes are.

Digging into the clutter can be a daunting process and can seem messy and chaotic. And it can be a never-ending process if you don't approach it with the goal of developing a new system rather than addressing symptoms. In his book *Getting Things Done: The Art of Stress-Free Productivity*, David Allen advocates getting all of our clutter out in the open before we start organizing. Allen's book is mostly about personal productivity at home and at work, but the principles he advocates on the individual level are not unlike what I'm proposing for the organizational level. The organization needs to throw all its clutter on the floor, empty all its metaphorical drawers, cupboards, and closets, and really see how much junk it has. Only when you see the entirety of what you're dealing with will you be able to identify the essential elements for making the organization run at peak performance and recognize those superfluous systems, processes, and practices that are impeding progress and performance.

Questions to identify unnecessary systems and processes:

- What does the customer want?
- Why does the customer want it?
- How have customer requirements changed in the last year? In the last three years?
- What are the fewest steps needed to benefit our customers?
- Who should be doing which steps?
- What are the actual steps we're doing today to deliver what the customer wants?
- Are we doing extra steps?
- Why are we doing extra steps?
- When did we start doing extra steps?
- Why did we start doing those extra steps *at that time*?
- How does this activity benefit the organization?
- What would happen if we stopped doing these extra steps?
- What do these extra steps prevent you (or someone else) from doing?
- What problems does management get involved in?

These questions will allow you to identify the systems that are essential and reliable and those that are not.

What Are the Elements of a Fearless Culture?

Many people think of leadership as the top of an organizational flow chart. Many also mistakenly think that a management role and leadership are one in the same. Still others think of leadership as a type of charisma or dynamism that drives an organization. I find these views of leadership to be flat. They define leadership one-dimensionally, either as position or as personality. Neither of these common perspectives makes room for leadership to occur in areas of an organization outside senior management or in functional roles.

After working with many organizations developing people and designing processes, my view is a bit deeper. Leadership can, does, and must happen in the Run, but for that to happen, the organization needs to develop a fearless culture on the front line.

A fearless culture is one in which top-performing individuals and/or departments inspire others to pursue higher standards of performance. Leadership is an intangible, interpersonal approach to organizational effectiveness. Whereas management is a function of improving systems and processes, leadership is a function of empowering people. Leadership is about unleashing the full potential of a person even when that person can't see her full potential. Organizations need both leadership and management to reach peak performance.

Run-Improve-Grow assumes that leadership is multidimensional. **Leadership** is an interpersonal development of trust and rapport that inspires a higher standard of performance. As such, leadership cannot be attained without an active relationship. Without mutual trust and confidence between two parties (individual and individual; individual and group; group and group), leadership cannot exist. And without leadership, Run-Improve-Grow cannot flourish.

So what traits must leaders possess to instill trust and confidence in their relationships with their employees?

- Empathy—compassion for and understanding of an employee's emotions and job assumptions, and recognition of what the employee must do to get the job done. Walk in her shoes for a day...

- Respect—a genuine appreciation for the innate talents of each individual and the work she does. It's a mind-set: treat each person with the respect she deserves.
- Nonjudgment—positive, open, and unbiased observation of an individual's ideas and performance.
- Humility—understanding that everyone makes mistakes, including yourself, but also understanding that everyone has great ideas and significant strengths.
- Calm—understanding that there is a solution for everything, and having the ability to step back and find the solution.

Leaders need to realize that they can't absolutely control people's performance, nor can they fully control external factors like market conditions, competitive forces, regulatory environments, and so on. They can only control the systems and processes they use and then influence employees' behaviors through leadership. Once leaders accept that fact, they will be able to direct their energies toward the right areas.

Managers and leaders fulfill different roles in the organization. We manage systems and we lead people. In Run-Improve-Grow, all frontline supervisors and mid-tier managers have both management and leadership responsibilities: they manage by designing and upgrading systems and processes; they lead by building confidence, inspiring performance improvements, and influencing Run execution. Managers employing Run-Improve-Grow can only drive performance to a certain point based on system and process efficiencies; only leaders can tap into an individual's personal motivations to drive performance to a higher standard. That is, leaders inspire their team to perform at higher levels—levels never considered realistic or even reasonable. In that way, leaders connect with people. By contrast, managers are overseers of work; they focus on process. That distinction is important because when managers try to control people, they drain energy instead of adding it.

What Are the Impediments to a Fearless Culture?

Surprisingly, what compromises new leaders' ability to control and influence operational change successfully often boils down to a series of bad decisions borne of bad judgment and convenience:

- Spending too much time on the wrong function
- Putting the wrong person in a position of leadership
- Devoting too much time to the wrong people

The first big impediment is spending too much time on the wrong function. It's hard to cultivate a leadership culture when individuals don't recognize their most-value-added function or they insist on doing other people's work. A mid-tier leader may be comfortable in the Run, but his most-value-added function is focusing on proactive Improvements. The marathon manager who is completely embedded in the Run is spending too much time in the wrong place. Whether you call it marathon management, micromanagement, or helicopter management, it all means the same thing: the manager is not doing his job. He's doing someone else's.

The second big impediment occurs when the wrong person is put in a position of leadership. Many organizations trap themselves by selecting the person with the greatest technical skills to fill a leadership role. Organizations often choose for leadership roles people who know a product well, fully understand operational intricacies, and can answer any and all questions about processes—regardless of their leadership potential or demonstrated leadership abilities. That's a shallow approach to leadership hiring. These people are nothing more than managers of convenience.

Managers with high technical skill but less leadership potential tend to be impatient with people who are less technically skilled than they are. The Run system has been built around their skills, and they're intolerant of anyone without the same expertise. They're short tempered and, ironically, unhelpful—the exact opposite of what an organization needs in a leader. When you hire or promote a manager for a leadership role and you find yourself wondering, "Why is this person not getting results?" think back to the time that you selected him. Was that person selected because of technical skills or because of leadership capabilities? In general, are you hiring managers or leaders? Are you making hiring decisions out of convenience or out of strategic concerns? Small variations in who is hired for what roles can cause significant disruptions (or benefits) to your final score.

The final impediment to developing a fearless culture is devoting too much time to the wrong people. What has society indicated we should do with poor performers? Remediate. When people don't get it, leaders feel obligated to help them. That's what leadership's all about, right? We're determined that our involvement and instruction make a difference. We mean well, but are we really doing what's best for the other members of the team?

In our organizations, some employees may not understand how to flawlessly execute their jobs, or they may seem incapable of mastering the job's functions. They can do nothing independently and need constant guidance. And they know it. At every turn they either ask for help or need you to check to ensure that what they did is okay. They are the organization's lowest performers. They're like the squeaky wheel on a shopping cart that draws your attention away from steering and causes you to crash into the banana stand.

Despite a manager's good intentions, focusing on the organization's squeaky wheels is detrimental to top performers, to overall performance, and to the organization's ability to raise its standards. Over years of analyzing how leaders interact with poor performers, I have noticed that when a leader focuses significant attention on problematic employees, higher-performing employees increasingly respond to issues in the same manner so as to garner their leader's attention. They save the day by solving urgent problems related to their poor-performing brethren and then make a lot of noise about how bad everyone else is. These top performers become increasingly frustrated as they try to grab their manager's attention. That's not at all what a successful Run requires! A successful Run cultivates the opposite situation, one in which leaders empower and enable top performers to set higher performance standards for others.

If cultivating top performers creates better results, why wouldn't leaders focus more heavily on employees who have proven they have the greatest potential, who have proactively implemented improvements, and who have demonstrated team commitment, rather than focusing on employees who haven't delivered on their promises to modify their behaviors, have required hand-holding, and have stubbornly reversed positive team energy and made it negative?

It seems so obvious, yet knowing all of this, managers still end up investing a disproportionate amount of time with poor performers or "draggers" instead of top performers. Frontline leaders like that create two problems. First, they incur opportunity costs related to other reactive improvement projects. Time spent managing the behaviors of draggers causes leaders to forego opportunities to find solutions for more significant operational issues. Second, they inadvertently hold back their top performers—and themselves. When leaders reward poor performers with their time, the message the frontline leader sends to higher-performing individuals is basically, "You're doing a great job, now stay where you are while everyone else catches up." Processes tend to be designed around the issues related to poor performers. Unfortunately, that slows down the rate of progress for top performers, who become frustrated (even irritated) working in unnecessarily complicated systems designed to compensate for mediocrity and low expectations. Any confidence top performers had in their leaders evaporates.

Why Getting to Fearless Matters

Eliminating marathon managers of any type is critical to your organization's overall success and long-term health. It's the only way to get to fearless. Relationships of trust create positive dividends throughout the organization. It's the polar opposite of a cynical cycle. In a trusting environment, employees are more likely to bring up ideas or share some other information that could be vitally important to future strategic and operational decision making. That willingness to bring up new ideas reflects courage.

When employees and managers have a trusting relationship, everyone is more inclined to share suggestions without fear of ridicule and rejection. People fearlessly put their ideas to the group for honest and rigorous consideration. The trust bond ensures that the ideas are scrutinized, not the people who advance them.

Moreover, when frontline employees themselves propose solutions, those employees become invested in the solutions. They seek to own the Run and the Improve processes both in the present and in the future. Let them. By implementing the suggestions advanced by the frontline workers, managers spark the front line's belief that its future suggestions will also be given significant consideration. Employees who see their managers' consideration are encouraged to be active participants in the organization. In short, frontline employees can *see* their value, and they become genuinely engaged.

For managers to effectively detach from the Run, they must have dual functions. One involves developing systems and processes, and the other involves developing people. To develop confident frontline personnel capable of owning the Run, managers have to transfer their knowledge of customer expectations, standards, systems, and processes to their frontline employees. Freed from the Run, managers can then focus on those positive, proactive improvements that help frontline employees handle new growth opportunities. Through system, process, and people development, managers (through leadership) serve as the integral bridge between the Run and the Grow.

TAKEAWAYS

- A fearless culture is impossible with marathon managers in place.
- We manage processes and lead people.
- To break out of a Run-centric culture, organizations must eliminate the need for the marathon manager and transition that manager firmly into the Improve.
- Identifying the most-value-added function of all team members and placing them in positions that maximize their strengths (and that value) is a critical step to eliminating marathon managers.
- Design systems around your top performers rather than your mediocre ones.
- Conceptualize systems as if they're for a one-person company, and resist anything that complicates these pure processes.
- Making reactive process improvements results in designing a new—and simpler—Run system that managers can turn over to the front line to lead.
- To definitively eliminate the need for managers to be embedded in the Run, an organization's leaders need to cultivate relationships based on honesty, respect, and trust with their employees.

3

Empower the Front Line to Lead: Move Over, Management

Transitioning leadership of the Run to the front line is rarely as easy as simply saying it needs to occur. If you've ever taught a teenager to drive, you understand what I'm saying. If you haven't, think back to what you had to go through when you were learning to drive.

Parents are the world's most generous chauffeurs. They spend years shuttling kids and their gear back and forth to school, play-dates, sports practices and games, music lessons, extracurricular activities, social events, and even dates. But as the kids reach driving age, the parent can't just stop driving and hand the keys over to the unlicensed, unschooled sixteen-year-old. The process that occurs to transfer responsibility and accountability for the teenager's transportation is painstaking and very uneven. There's likely a lot of gasping and yelling, "Stop! Look out!!!" Yet at the same time, parents must practice patience, remain calm, and adhere to a firm commitment to the right skills, processes, and rules of the road. The ultimate goal of the parent-chauffeur is to eliminate her role as chauffeur by creating a completely independent, confident, reliable, responsible driver whom the parent, and other drivers, can trust on the road.

Eliminating the marathon manager from the Run is not unlike taking the parent-chauffeur out of household transportation duties. The goal is not to dump responsibility in the lap of the front line and then dash to an office to start thinking of improvement opportunities. Effective leaders want to transition responsibilities so that the front line is always capable of undertaking them. (That builds confidence.) *Then* leaders can start planning proactive improvements for the front line's systems and processes.

How Do You Develop a Fearless Culture in the Run?

Surmounting the impediments to creating a fearless culture in the Run isn't as difficult as you might be thinking. There are three very practical ways to shape the leadership culture you want to pervade the Run:

- Raise the bar of excellence by investing in top performers and removing obstacles that frustrate them.
- Foster quick-win success by removing frustrations and making meaningful changes quickly to bolster team confidence, enthusiasm, and trust.
- Implement daily huddles to foster a positive "what went well" environment, communicate your standards of performance, and create a simple touch point for communicating status of reactive improvements.

Raise the Bar of Excellence

Recall that leadership is an interpersonal development of trust and rapport that inspires a higher standard of performance. So, to foster a fearless front line, leaders need to shift from spending too much time with the wrong people, the organization's worst and neediest employees to the right people, the organization's top performers. Frontline leaders can rekindle the motivation of disenchanted top performers with a simple shift of attention and simple actions like pursuing their suggestions and publicly giving them credit for their ideas. Who gets the lion's share of a leader's attention has great impact on the organization—the full impact can be explained by a concept called 10-80-10, which applies to not only individuals, but to cross-functional teams and even entire business units.

In my experience, employees in every department of every organization can be segmented in the following way:

- 10 percent performers
- 80 percent followers
- 10 percent draggers

Top performers are just that: those employees who consistently excel at their most-value-added functions. Top performers take initiative without being told what to do because they are naturally driven to excellence. Flawed performance irritates top performers. On a front line, the influence of top performers is critical to a team's development of higher performance standards.

Followers are the majority. They have a genuine desire to perform well, but they simply need a model to follow to raise the bar of excellence. Followers seek to emulate the behaviors and attitudes of their top-performing peers, so the more top performers are put in front of the group and the more attention those top performers are given, the more followers will rise to achieve higher performance levels.

Draggers are low-performing individuals inspired to change only when absolutely necessary—and maybe not even then. They are often the absolute skeptics of the group. They are stubbornly opposed to change. The most intractable dragger may not change even when the risk of not adapting is being left behind (becoming irrelevant or being demoted or terminated).

To better understand how top performers affect an organization's performance, look at the figure below.

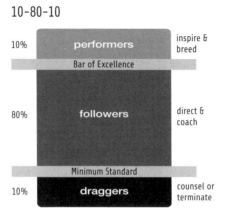

Figure 3.1

The figure reflects the 10-80-10 composition of the total employee population grouped according to performance standards. Consider this the status quo of an average organization. In an organization dealing with marathon managers, a fear-based culture, loss of top performers, and ineffective systems, the overall performance level drops, as shown by the figure below.

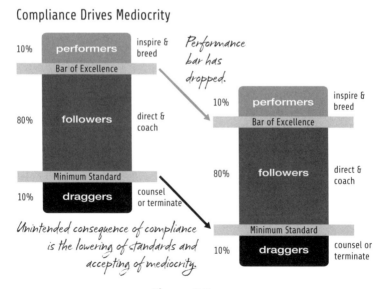

Figure 3.2

Too often, managers begin to reduce their standards to account for their lower performers. Managers may begin to add new procedures, double checks, policies, and so forth to combat the poor performers. These managers may have good intentions, but all too often the new systems are counterproductive, as they reduce the performance of top performers. These processes put speed humps in the way of those most capable of succeeding. While hoping to improve overall performance, managers actually create a model for mediocrity and promote consistency rather than excellence. Top performers begin to adopt an attitude of "Okay, you want me to do it that way, fine!" When this happens, top performers become disenchanted and unmotivated and dip into the follower territory of, say, B-level performance. They still strive for excellence, but they adapt to their flawed system. Similarly, those followers who had been performing at B levels slip to a mediocre C, and those followers who had been at C slip to D. The result is a downward shift in performance for the entire staff.

If, however, frontline leaders have spent time removing the frustrations and the obstacles of their top performers, the results are the opposite. These leaders are able to succeed by listening to, developing, influencing, and empowering top performers. When this happens, performance standards shift higher, as depicted in the figure below. The strong focus on excellence pulls the followers at the B level into the A game, and the followers at the C level up to the B level, and so on. Therefore, we refer to 10-80-10 in the Run-Improve-Grow system as "raising the bar of excellence."

Removing Obstacles Drives Excellence

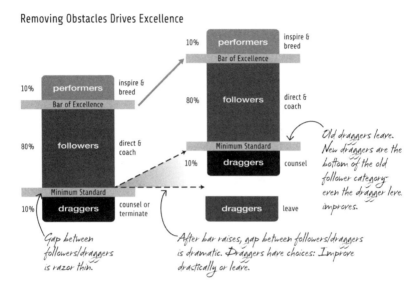

Figure 3.3

In my experience, the only way for a frontline team to consistently raise its performance standards and avoid a performance sawtooth effect is through its top performers. Thinking in terms of the 10-80-10 diagrams in figures 3.1–3.3, that means the leader needs to consistently invest more time with top performers to shift the performance of followers upward.

Now, I'm not saying the lowest performers should be ignored. What I'm advocating is that a frontline leader invest the majority of her time empowering her top performers rather than trying to remediate the draggers. The rationale is simple: frontline top performers have a unique advantage in team development. As peers of the other frontline workers, top performers have already established relationships with their coworkers. They're in the trenches together, so to speak. Perhaps the top performers have already stepped in to assist draggers in improving their performance, or maybe they've had an inspiring impact on followers. When a front line's top performers are free to naturally pursue excellence, their actions and behaviors become a standard for the followers and draggers.

If you still need to be convinced that reallocating your attention to top performers is the key to increasing performance, answer this question: If you were to start your own company today, who would you take from your current organization and why? When I ask this question at speaking engagements, most people say they would take talented, top-performing individuals from a variety of backgrounds. Rightfully so. Sustainable organizations are born from top performers in many areas reaching peak performance as a team. You probably have a gut-level feel for who the top performers in your organization are. Sometimes they stand out. Other times, not so much. So how do you tell the top performers from the draggers?

That's easy. Top performers have three tells that give them away. First, top performers tend to ask penetrating questions. They have high levels of intellectual curiosity and are committed to seeking and finding ways to add more value. Typically, top performers gather information through questions—specifically, questions that seek progress.

Note that draggers also tend to ask a lot of questions, but the difference between the questions posed by draggers and those posed by top performers is the tone and the intent. Draggers are negative and ask argumentative questions, whereas top performers' questions are solutions oriented.

Another way to identify top performers is by the natural respect they receive from their peers. Top performers are viewed as *the* individuals to go to within the group if there is an issue that needs clarification or a peer who needs help.

Finally, top performers are doers. They deliver on their promises and act on their ideas. That's why people, especially peers, look to them for answers. They're the people who seize the opportunity to make the changes they've been wanting to make for years. Anyone in an organization can *talk* about an improvement idea; it is the ones who *act* who stand out. By taking quick action in the early stages of a Run-Improve-Grow transformation, top performers influence the beliefs, attitudes, and behaviors of their peers to create a new standard of excellence.

One of the most successful methods of raising the bar of excellence is enlisting top performers to share their techniques, processes, and best practices with the entire team. Early in my career, I had the opportunity to test my theory. I had been put in charge of a production team with outstanding but very inconsistent results. After collecting some baseline performance measurements, I discovered that the team produced an average of thirty-seven units per hour. The two top performers in the group, however, achieved fifty-eight and sixty units per hour, whereas our lowest performer was producing only twenty units per hour. The performance disparity across the front line was too wide to ignore.

Because we were in the medical device industry, we had procedures that made it very clear how to execute each and every step of production. In theory, there should have been no variability in the way people did their jobs. In practice, there were as many ways as there were people. I enlisted the top two performers to show the rest of the 50-employee team their production technique. Immediately, the draggers in the group began to throw up roadblocks, saying that going faster would risk the product quality. Fortunately, we had measured the in-process defect rate, and the person with the lowest defect rates was—you guessed it—the person who had the highest production rate.

After one week of this training, the team began producing an average of forty-three units per hour. In the subsequent months, the average team rate rose to fifty-one units an hour. What was most shocking was that the top two performers didn't stand still. Their performance improved to seventy-five and eighty units per hour in the same time frame! That was a 37 percent improvement.

Foster Quick-Win Success

Sometimes, finding an improvement area that galvanizes the team is not so easy. The key to positioning talent with the right skills, strengths, and behaviors is identifying a uniform objective toward which everyone can work. A team-building exercise called a **quick win** is one such uniform objective.

Quick wins solve problems rapidly to remove chronic frustrations. They are initiatives intended to spark confidence and trust by tackling obstacles that have become institutionalized. The most successful quick wins are those that resolve the problems people have been managing around on a daily basis.

At one ornamental design company, the front line was managing around a large corrugated decking platform that was smack in the middle of the floor, dividing the front line's work space in two. It was such an obstruction that, during the winter months, the team would have to open the dock doors to maneuver large projects around the decking. Few actually knew why the decking was placed like that, but many assumed that the company president wanted the decking there for a reason.

As it happened, the company president only wanted the decking inside to keep it out of the elements and prevent it from rusting. As long as the decking was protected, he didn't care where it was stored. Finding a new location to store the decking became the team's first quick-win project. When the RIG project leader asked the front line what it could get done if the decking were moved by the following week, the team began talking about all the projects it could complete earlier than anticipated.

Energized by that spark, the team came in that Saturday to clear out an outdoor storage area and design and prepare materials to build a roof to cover it. Within five days, the decking had been moved to a protected space outside.

Generally speaking, quick wins like that one are intended to create an experience that changes frontline beliefs and serves as a model to raise the bar of excellence. Quick wins provide a vision of how to work together as a team to further an organization's overall vision. So, when teams organize around an improvement effort that can be achieved with almost guaranteed success and in a relatively short time frame, team members experience near-instant gratification for their efforts. Speed is important because it creates positive, winning momentum and team camaraderie. Think about it: nothing builds camaraderie more quickly and effectively than winning momentum.

The energy created by quick wins brings coworkers together in a collaborative mind-set. As frontline teams develop their own quick-win momentum, they can spread their experience, enthusiasm, and energy to other frontline departments and their leaders and employees. The team mentality soon becomes the spark that ignites other teams to raise the bar of excellence across the entire organization.

Choosing the right quick-win opportunity is, therefore, quite important. Believe it or not, you've probably already got a list of possible opportunities right in front of you. The same list of obstacles that prevent a marathon manager from detaching from the Run is basically a list of opportunities for quick wins. By removing obstacles in the Run, frontline and mid-tier leaders can begin to cultivate Run-Improve-Grow throughout the organization.

Starting in the Run, leaders must prioritize possible initiatives according to a set of specific criteria. Applying these criteria to opportunities ensures that the selected initiatives are the ones most likely to spark confidence among individuals and across departments:

- Likelihood of success—quick-win projects must affect the beliefs and behaviors of frontline employees, so they must have a strong (or almost guaranteed) likelihood of success.
- Visible symbol of success—quick-win projects must visibly solve a problem so frontline employees can see its value.
- Scalability—quick-win projects must provide an example of how to create a new improvement standard among other individuals and in other departments.
- Teamwork model—quick-win projects must provide an example of how to bring people together toward a common goal.
- Customer confidence focus—quick-win projects must work to improve customer confidence.
- Management leadership model—quick-win projects must be significant enough to align management systems and leadership behaviors to a fearless front line.

Selected projects that support your Run-Improve-Grow road map may not fall into all categories. If that's the case, then jump on the quick wins that are symbolic to frontline workers. Those types of quick wins can have a significant positive psychological impact and thereby create a supportive environment in which the next quick wins can launch successfully.

Be careful not to gravitate toward performance-based projects whose *only* impact is to immediately bolster short-term financial results. Instead, strategically select quick wins that will remove frustrations and inspire action. Those are the ones that will add the most value for long-term organizational sustainability and growth. Tackling projects that are symbolic to frontline workers demonstrates caring and concern for those workers. Their needs matter. Performance-based initiatives satisfy the needs of the company more than the needs of the employee. That's why symbolic projects are so critical. They represent the people part of the equation.

Implement Daily Huddles

Quick-win projects form the connective tissue between management and leadership. Management involves refining the organization's systems and processes to an efficient perfection. A project that satisfies the quick-win criteria will inherently involve system and process improvement. Yet instead of marathon managers implementing the solutions, the employees themselves do the heavy lifting—that's where leadership and management connect.

Leadership and management also connect in the **daily huddle**, a forum where leaders can change the type of conversation they have with their employees. Every day at a set time, all members of the frontline team, including the frontline leader, congregate in the same location to openly discuss daily Run topics, daily and general Run performance objectives, and reactive improvement suggestions and plans.

Daily huddles produce three outcomes:

• Behavior modeling
• Communication in a common language
• Raised bar of excellence

These three outcomes occur in the process of identifying and executing quick-win projects. Huddles should provide more than enough quick-win opportunities, as long as frontline leaders (and top performers) ask the right questions and gather the right data. In my experience, the simplest and most effective question leaders use to uncover quick-win opportunities is, "What are your biggest obstacles on a daily basis?" Many of the most immediate frontline quick wins come from removing clear obstacles that have made simple procedures unnecessarily complicated. Think back to the ornamental design company and the decking platform in the middle of the shop floor. An obvious—and enormous—obstacle was immediately identified and called out by the simple question about what prevented the team's Run from performing at its peak. When frontline employees describe in detail the obstacles that have been preventing flawless Run execution, they provide raw data for a frontline leader to plan a quick win fearlessly and open a space for modeling new behavior.

Each interaction a leader has with her team is an opportunity for her to shape her front line's personal beliefs, set new standards of performance, and develop her team's problem-solving skills. So in the daily huddle, leaders need to be cognizant of the types of questions they're asking and how. They are modeling new behavior for future leaders. Leaders may know what their front line needs to work on, but the true benefits come when the front line itself begins to recognize and then anticipate what it needs to work on. The leader shouldn't do the work for the team—doing so robs the team members of an opportunity to grow.

The second outcome of daily huddles is a common language. That can be achieved by focusing on two simple yet powerful standards: what went well (WWW) and what needs improvement (WNI).

Start first by focusing on what went well. That reinforces the positive value of employees' daily behaviors in the Run. It confirms the value of their efforts. It also allows employees to transmit to their coworkers information related to strong performance; that, in turn, is a way to set new standards.

Against the positive backdrop of what went well, employees

can confidently focus on what needs improvement from a more critical, neutral mind-set. Without creating a positive context, examining what needs improvement could be seen only as an indictment of poor performance, especially in a group setting.

Addressing topics in that order—what went well followed by what needs improvement—takes the group off the defensive and lets employees voice areas they recognize as needing improvement. It's a self-reinforcing system of communication that keeps the concept of raising the bar of excellence at the forefront, because what went well is about respect and a position of self-confidence.

To further reinforce new behaviors, daily huddles should occur in the same place each day. Having an assigned and collective space for this purpose is invaluable because it creates a tangible cue for teamwork and collaboration. A dedicated space is also likely to become a communication hub for the group beyond the time of the daily huddle. Employees may meet there throughout the day to exchange ideas, work on solutions, or simply get information.

The central fixture in the daily huddle space is the huddle board. Huddle boards signify the group's central collaboration point and serve as a visual reminder of important information. Run-Improve-Grow huddle boards are generally divided into three sections. The top two-thirds of the board contain the upcoming week's schedule, organized in a fashion appropriate to the type of work the organization does. The bottom third of the board is divided vertically into left and right halves. The bottom left segment of the board keeps track of what went well, and the bottom right segment keeps track of ideas and suggestions for what needs improvement.

Run-Improve-Grow huddle boards are as symbolic as they are tactical. The information changes often, so the board acts like a team news feed. It keeps the entire team updated on actual progress and opportunities for progress. The board is also a tangible reminder of the organization's commitment to success and high performance. The list of what went well provides employees with a visual reminder of success. The list of what needs improvement is a visual reminder of what remains to be done and prevents a satisfied, complacent attitude from creeping back into the front line. The items on those lists are constantly changing, analogous to running water. Running water is healthier than stagnant water, so, to prevent your team from becoming frustrated and unhealthy, the lists of what went well and what needs improvement shouldn't sit there too long before being refreshed. And just like healthy inventory turnover indicates a healthy sales cycle, consistent turnover of what went well and what needs improvement indicates that higher standards of performance are being met and sustained.

In addition to providing visual progress reminders to the team, the huddle board also acts as a schedule reminder that keeps the team thinking about priorities. The weekly schedule is regularly updated, so employees have a view of what needs to be done that day as well as over the course of the next four. The huddle board gives a visual of the organization's pipeline and what needs to be done to keep the front line running the operations reliably.

So, who actually leads these daily huddles? Ultimately, the frontline leader will be the one to lead the huddle. Before that happens, however, the frontline leader will need to be coached by a masterful trainer. That person may be someone inside or outside the organization, but either way, the trainer needs to regularly practice the behaviors that you want the frontline leader to model to the rest of the team.[1] Just like any other job training, the frontline leader needs to be trained in the skills needed to lead the huddle. Keep in mind the purpose of the huddles within Run-Improve-Grow: modeling behavior, communicating in a common language, and raising the bar of excellence. If mid-tier and frontline leaders only possess manager characteristics, they need a forum where they can see how to act like leaders. The daily huddle is a great opportunity. When mid-tier managers see their frontline leaders embrace proper leadership behaviors, the mid-tier managers can pass along responsibility for the huddles to frontline leaders and so on to the front line's top performers.

Recall the 10-80-10 diagrams on how the frontline leader affects the direction of the frontline employees' performance. The goal is not to drop the responsibility on the front line (or its top performers) then dash to a corner office to develop master strategies independently. The frontline leader needs to begin the process and set the example for how the huddle should be conducted. Then, as top performers are empowered and take ownership of their processes, frontline leaders can step out of the way and transition daily huddle ownership to them. A successful transition depends on a strong first example. Frontline leaders must fearlessly establish a daily huddle routine before they can effectively pass ownership along to frontline top performers.

When frontline leaders introduce huddles to their frontline employees, don't be surprised if at first few participate out of fear of embarrassment or rejection. Some may think they're going to sound or look stupid in front of their peers; others may think their ideas won't be accepted. Frontline employees need to develop intra-huddle trust (fearlessness). They need to know that no idea is stupid and every comment is respected and appreciated. They can develop those beliefs by watching their leaders practice courage, honest and transparent communication, and curiosity. The first huddle is the place to wipe the slate clean, start new habits, and establish new precedents for relationships between you and your manager and between you and your employees, among the employees, and between everyone and the work. This can be challenging because many of us are conditioned to point out what's going wrong before we discuss what's going right. We want to identify problems so we can fix them (or, depending on the person, harp on them). Putting discussions of what's going well first is critical to building a successful huddle and creating new group norms that use successes as a foundation for improvement.

In the course of establishing new norms, frontline leaders need to engage top performers to extend that simple invitation to participate. From my experience, as top performers are engaged, that engagement sparks confidence in others who then become more willing to voice their opinions and ideas during the second or third week of huddles. The more involved and invested everyone on the team becomes, followers and draggers (often the most cynical of the bunch) build confidence in themselves and in the group. Over the years, numerous experiences have convinced me that huddles truly simplify management activities. Many hands make light work. When your entire team is involved and engaged, they become stakeholders in their outcomes and the responsibility for those outcomes is shared.

How Do You Transition Leadership to Top Performers?

Think back to the teen driving example that opened the chapter. Transitioning the responsibility for transportation to the teen driver doesn't happen instantaneously. In fact, it doesn't happen until both the state and the parents say the teen is ready and capable of driving alone. Getting to that handoff involves many layers of development and formation, and not surprisingly, the learning actually starts with the parents and how *they* drive.

Although this example is simplified, our organizations transition leadership somewhat similarly. The foundation of learning what to do or how to act comes from behavior modeling, the core of the employee development process in Run-Improve-Grow.

There is an old saying: water seeks its own level. Whatever behavior and attitudes top leaders and mid-level leaders demonstrate, those same behaviors will be repeated—if not amplified—throughout the organization. To prepare the front line's top performers to take a leadership role for the Run, the top leaders in the organization need to be modeling the exact behaviors and attitudes they want those top performers to emulate. Collaborative and consultative behavior essential to Run-Improve-Grow reconnects the top of the organization to the estranged front line and surrounds everyone with a culture of respect and consideration.

Behavioral modeling creates the environment in which direct training occurs. Top performers may be technically skilled, but leadership also requires people skills and conceptual skills. Because the behaviors required of leaders are fairly straightforward (courage, curiosity, honesty, authenticity, respect), people may bristle at the suggestion that they're not doing them right or at all. Let them know that you don't mean to imply that they can't do those things. Leadership simply requires them to practice those behaviors on a more consistent and concerted basis.

Give your employees language that reinforces leadership behavior. For example, questions phrased as "Why do you do that?" or "Why did you…?" can put an employee on the defensive. Instead, consider the following alternatives:

- "What prevents us from doing…?"
- "What's causing us to need to…?"
- "How is it that we need to…?"
- "What happens that causes the need for…?"
- "What occurred that caused us to think we need to…?"
- "What occurred that caused your thinking to change about…?"

Phrasing questions in this manner focuses the probing on the activity, the action, and the situation and takes the focus of the probing off the employee and her intentions. It's a subtle difference, to be sure, but making this change is important. People are much more open to suggestion when they understand why a topic or issue is important.

Always asking "Why did you do this?" and "Why did you do that?" influences the way an employee feels about the relationship. Open and honest relationships are what we're after, and putting those around us on the defensive is not the way to get there. Similarly, those phrases implicitly set up an interpersonal hierarchy, where the one asking is superior and the one being asked is inferior. That is not how you want to educate your front line to lead. You'll end up with people either acting like petty dictators or not thinking for themselves and waiting to be told what to do.

Behavior modeling is tacit teaching. It occurs without directly calling attention to what's being taught. Educating is explicit teaching. It *does* call attention directly to what's being taught, so in this phase of developing your employees to lead, you need to not only use the questioning phrases above regularly, you also need to let your employees know what you're doing and why you're doing it. Consider carving out a place in the huddle area to post a list of respectful question phrases, like those above, as a visual cue during the huddle and throughout the day. Employees who need or want a quick reminder can look to the list and put the focus back on the problems, not on personalities.

All of the above assumes the frontline employees are technically skilled and only need leadership development. As you start tackling the opportunities for quick wins, you may discover that there are frontline employees with technical skill deficiencies. Maybe those employees were never shown how to do the job properly (perhaps they were trained by a dragger or maybe the tasks were not properly designed to ensure a reliable outcome); maybe they came to the organization with skill deficits from poor-quality education. Regardless of the reason, you'll need to identify skill deficits and make plans to fill them. It will be difficult for employees to take control of the Run if a significant portion of the team is inept. Just as behavior modeling is the foundation of education, education provides the foundation for delegating responsibilities.

With a front line that has technical savvy and has begun to internalize the practice of the leadership behaviors, you're ready to begin empowering your team. The idea of empowerment in Run-Improve-Grow is not a condescending, now-it's-your-problem kind of delegating. Instead, it's empowerment built on the principle of most-added-value functions and the assumption that everyone wants to make a meaningful contribution. People want to be valued and to find meaning in their work, so let them.

You may encounter a situation where empowerment comes naturally, with the fearless front line seizing responsibility rather than being given it. In those cases, the frontline team often takes the initiative because it's confident in its ability to succeed. And it's willing to be accountable because it believes it can control the new process and therefore control the outcome.

Just because frontline employees are ready to take the mantle of responsibility for the Run, it doesn't mean there will not be bumps in the road, however. Think about the teenage driver. The parent-chauffeur doesn't want to wait until the teenager has the same level of experience as she does, nor does she want to wait until the teenager is a perfect and supremely confident driver. She turns the keys over when he's a good, solid, capable driver she can have confidence in. For managers in the Run, it's comparable. They need to pass their keys to an energized front line waiting to journey on its own. As soon as the front line has demonstrated it's on the road to full leadership practice—and has made some good progress down that road—it's time to trust and detach.

"Detach" doesn't mean cut loose. Employees in a new path with new responsibilities need mentoring. The guidance a mentor provides creates an invisible safety net for an employee's self-confidence and provides a way to save face as he works to internalize leadership behaviors. Mentors are people to whom confounded employees can go to talk through ideas—the good, the bad, and the ugly. Considering different options and scenarios before taking action on a problem or challenge is good practice. Running through the full range of possibilities with a mentor before deciding how to proceed helps the fledgling leader solidify his thinking and embrace his own style.

A mentor knows her role involves educating and guiding, not performing for (or in place of) the mentee. Mentors do not control the work of the mentee. The mentor is someone with a higher level of skill in areas the mentee is trying to develop.

Regular contact with a mentor is what helps the mentee solidify his new behaviors. As your organization moves into this phase of Run-Improve-Grow, consider having mentors and mentees get together for a weekly or biweekly improvement plan review. To keep the focus of the thirty- to forty-five-minute meeting on leadership development, the mentee should complete a short form with six open-ended topics:

- Special concerns the mentee wants to discuss during the meeting
- Accomplishments since the previous meeting (this is akin to what went well)
- Insights the mentee had and decisions or choices the mentee made since the previous meeting

- What the mentee intended to do but didn't get done
- Challenges the mentee is facing
- Opportunities open to the mentee[2]

Having the mentee answer these questions will give shape and purpose to the meetings and ensure that the meetings are a fruitful time of connection between the mentor and the mentee. The form also gives the mentee space to take a moment to detach from the Run and reflect on how things are going. In that way, the form acts as a tool for developing both people and conceptual skills.

As another means of mentoring top performers to become effective leaders, Run-Improve-Grow encourages a concept called try-storming. Try-storming is a leadership mechanism focused on taking quick action without the certainty of success—experimenting for learning and progress. The value of try-storming is to learn from an effort's results. An effort is only a failure if nothing has been learned from collective experiences and mistakes. Try-storming is prevalent in a Run-Improve-Grow because you're doing things that you've never done before. The best way to find out if something works is to try it—and if it doesn't work, learn from what happened, refine the process, and try again! A mentoring relationship can help the mentee objectively make sense of success and failure from someone who has been in her shoes before.

Mentoring is the final stage in the transition arc that ends with frontline employees leading the Run. It often results in personal development for the employee as well as collective growth for the organization. Getting to this stage of personal and organizational development is what positions the organization to move into the next phase of the RIG model—the Improve.

Why Transitioning Leadership to the Fearless Front Line Matters

Until your organization can turn leadership of the Run over to the front line, you will be wasting more management resources than you can reasonably account for. Think about it: all the time your managers spend in the Run working with the front line on reactive improvements is time those same managers are not working on proactive improvements or growth opportunities. And all that time meddling in the Run creates an environment of learned helplessness at the level where you most need confident, capable reliability.

For your organization to move from Run to Improve and ultimately to Grow, those managers with a more panoramic view of capabilities, markets, and future possibilities need to be freed up to turn those possibilities into realities. The only way to do that is to transition leadership for the Run to the fearless front line. Leave the day-to-day execution at the right level of the organization, and align your people with their most-value-added functions. Someone hired as a manager of a bakery is hired to manage the bakery, *not* bake the cakes. But without a fantastic baker, the manager is going to be hamstrung trying to grow the company. The roles work together—and need each other—so you've got to make sure you don't have all your resources trying to fulfill one single role in the organization. Until you can ensure a rock-solid, reliable Run, you're not going to be able to Grow, much less get out of the kitchen.

TAKEAWAYS

- Organizations need both leadership and management to achieve their greatest success.
- Leadership requires an active relationship.
- Good leaders are empathetic, respectful, nonjudgmental, humble, and calm. Leaders inspire their associates to perform at higher levels; managers control a front line's systems and processes and ultimately assist the frontline employees in taking ownership of those same systems and processes.

(continued)

- Three fundamental impediments to developing leadership are spending time on the wrong function, putting the wrong person in a position, and spending too much time with draggers.

- Overcoming these impediments and developing a culture of leadership involves raising the bar of excellence, fostering quick-win success, and implementing daily huddles.

- The composition of any organization is generally 10 percent top performers, 80 percent followers, and 10 percent draggers.

- Managers who spend too much time with draggers actually drag down the performance of followers and top performers, but managers who spend more time with top performers can raise the performance of draggers and followers.

- Quick action is a way to build individual confidence within a group setting. Quick wins are an offshoot of quick action and build confidence and momentum among employees.

- Quick wins provide a vision of how to work together as a team.

- Daily huddles provide the collective space for teams to identify obstacles to their peak performance, to review what went well and what needs improvement, and to discuss how to go about doing what needs to be done.

- Managers start daily huddles, but over time, top performers become the leaders, resulting in peer-led meetings.

- Transitioning leadership from managers to top performers starts by creating the desired environment through behavior modeling, then educating and mentoring new leaders as they develop their skills.

IMPROVE

LIBERATING LEADERS TO
DO THEIR BEST WORK

4

Transfer the Winning Momentum: Ignite the Spark

Nothing builds team camaraderie more quickly and effectively than winning momentum. Unfortunately, nothing is easier (or worse) than losing momentum. Systems heat up, people get fired up, positive energy is released, changes occur, and in the process, energy is dispersed. Just like systems in the natural world, organizations are subject to entropy.

After a successful quick-win project, a leader's challenge is to keep energy in the system so that employees stay engaged and the new behaviors become unconscious and establish the new baseline performance standards. Now that you've had this success from the quick win, you have a very narrow window of opportunity to make bold changes. If you wait for complete across-the-board buy-in before capitalizing on the quick win, the energy you've created will dissipate. That's because waiting for everyone to be on board with a change is unrealistic. You might as well not do anything.

But you must. Before you began transforming the Run, your organization probably looked something like this:

Figure 4.1

All the functions were distinct, and each was working at a similar level. RIG starts at a department or work-group level, so what does the organization look like after one department starts removing obstacles through quick wins? Something like this:

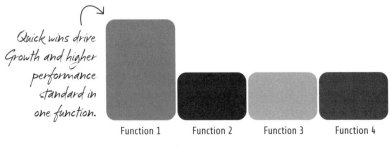

Quick wins drive Growth and higher performance standard in one function.

Figure 4.2

The performance of the group implementing RIG principles and tactics grows significantly in comparison to the other functional areas that have not been using RIG. In order to make real sustainable change, you need something like this to happen:

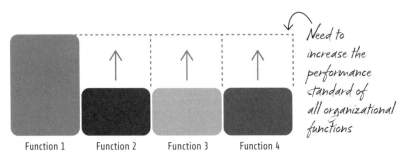

Need to increase the performance standard of all organizational functions

Figure 4.3

All functions need to increase their performance so that the level is higher across the entire organization. Leaders must drive new behaviors deeper into the function where Run-Improve-Grow started and then out across the breadth of the organization. The organization needs to raise the bar in a sustainable and perpetual way. But how does that actually happen?

It happens when someone models the change behaviors and starts taking action instead of watching and waiting for something to happen. Why can't that someone be you? Change really starts at the individual level and the spark spreads throughout the organization. You can be that catalyst. You *should* be that catalyst. You hold the key to transferring momentum to other people, departments, and functional areas.

Simple physics tells us that a body in motion wants to stay in motion, and sustained motion is the goal of a Run-Improve-Grow organization—to become a perpetual system that looks outside, then inside, to continuously drive the right behavior automatically with little management intervention. That's not easy. But you've got to do it.

Why Does the Momentum Usually Start in Operations?

Often, organizations target their operations department for a quick win (i.e., their momentum) before other frontline functions such as marketing, IT, HR, product development, customer service, and sales. Why does operations take priority?

Operations tends to be the starting point for quick wins because operations departments generally have more concrete standards, which makes it easier to define problems. (Departments outside of operations tend to lack established standards, so the quick-win model can create a model for other functions to follow.) Operations departments are also selected to launch quick wins because of those departments' importance to the Run. Literally, the Run can't function without operations, regardless of industry or organization. A hospital can't Run without its nurses, orderlies, and lab technicians; a restaurant can't Run without its chefs and wait staff; a manufacturing organization can't Run without its machinists, welders, buyers, fork truck drivers, and schedulers. That's not to say that non-operations departments or divisions don't play a role in quick wins. They do.

The key is operational optimization. For example, in a manufacturing company, sales and operations must be in sync so promises to customers are kept; purchasing and manufacturing must be in sync to reduce time, errors, and costs, and thus prices for customers; marketing and engineering must be in sync to innovate new products and services for the customer. Top-performing operations individuals and departments don't raise the bar of excellence in a vacuum. They bring along ancillary divisions, so once an entire operation has optimized its Run, a capstone or high-profile success can serve as a model for cross-functional teamwork.

What Are Some Common Roadblocks to Momentum?

Multiple obstacles will arise when you try to convert a successful quick win into deeper and broader organizational momentum. One main roadblock to converting momentum occurs when whatever improvement came from the quick win didn't really simplify anything. It may have achieved some numeric goal, like cycle-time reduction or increased percentage of on-time delivery or fewer defects, but perhaps it made no lasting improvement. Worse is when the quick win didn't actually solve the problem that was really the issue or remove all of the frustrations holding your team back day after day.

Another reason momentum from a quick win doesn't travel through an organization is that the win was achieved through extraordinary efforts, say by throwing more of the same resources at the problem. There's no way to maintain those exceptional circumstances on a regular basis, so whatever improvement they created can't be replicated.

Similarly, if, during the quick-win process, senior leaders made decisions and removed obstacles *for* the team, then the team hasn't learned any skills to help it remove its own obstacles going forward. The front line or the frontline supervisor never became empowered or took ownership, so when the senior leader is no longer involved, the front line can't solve the problems like the senior leader did. Quick wins are the low-hanging fruit. Once all the low-hanging fruit has been picked, there's only high-hanging fruit left. The next level of improvements is more challenging to implement. There's no model to follow. Plus, more complex problems require multifunctional teams to solve them, and if the team isn't ready for that, well, the momentum from all the quick wins is lost.

Perhaps what drove the quick win was a crisis situation. The team was in reactive mode, so the momentum stopped after the crisis was averted. Once there's no longer a crisis, the team goes back to being in stable condition until the next crisis. Or the opposite could be true: there's no sense of organizational urgency. Individuals don't feel that transferring the momentum across functions is that important. Maybe those who have participated in successful quick wins feel that other teams in the organization aren't being held to the new higher standards like they are (after they've raised the bar).

The most common reason that the energy from the quick win doesn't permeate the organization deep and wide and create new behavior, however, is that the leader didn't change how she led. Doing so is absolutely critical, so we'll spend all of chapter 6 addressing how to do just that.

Leaders who let their workers tiptoe into an improvement effort offer them an opportunity to bail out at the slightest level of discomfort or the smallest obstacle or problem they're unwilling or unable to solve. Instead of slowly stepping into a quick-win improvement project, leaders must model quick action to spark confidence in all employees. Recall the ornamental design company. What do you think the odds of success would have been if they had been allowed three weeks to relocate the decking? Three weeks can be an eternity. Think about all of the new projects and ideas that have come your way in the last three weeks. What have you put off in that time that has stayed in your to-do pile?

When the frontline leaders commit to modeling quick action, they eliminate easy excuses to quit and don't give their frontline employees time to dwell on a project's purpose and likelihood of success. Quick action lets a front line *live* its success. For the front line to be committed, they must feel supported by their leadership. The typical reaction of a front line that doesn't feel supported is, "We already tried to improve our lead times, and it didn't work." That's what they *say*. What they really *mean* is, "Unless you get *everyone* committed, don't waste your time; don't waste our time—and don't frustrate us with distractions."

Treating Quick Wins Like a Project

For organizations not committed to a complete Run-Improve-Grow journey, the goal is simply the quick win. After it's realized, there's nothing more to do. In this project-oriented mind-set, the euphoria from collective accomplishment evaporates almost instantly. Letting that momentum die allows skepticism and cynicism to creep back into the collective psyche. Top performers become demotivated, as their efforts fail to translate to something new and better or prompt additional and new improvement (a new standard of performance).[1] The system then shuts down, and starting it back up again requires even more effort from leaders than it did the first time around.

If organizations don't act quickly after a single quick win—or series of wins—the initial improvement to the Run will become no more than an isolated improvement project and may actually prevent real and lasting change from occurring. Change is hard and ultimately unsuccessful because:

- change programs are applied unequally in the organization;
- change programs have too broad a scope;

- goals of the change programs are mediocre; or
- change programs turn over with high frequency (which indicates lack of staying power).

At this point, I'd like to amend that list by adding:

- change programs have too narrow a scope.

I realize that I may sound a bit like Goldilocks, first saying the change is too broad and then saying the change is too narrow, but such is the case. In the context of momentum, the too-narrow scope limits the transfer of momentum from quick wins.

Most change programs can be described as targeted change models that focus on only one area, function, task, role, process, system, or procedure. In that way, they amount to getting only one part of the house in order. Targeted change models focus on one of four problems:

- Complex and unreliable processes
- Frontline leadership deficits
- Functional silos that create frustration and minimize performance
- Unpredictable growth that happens by default rather than by design

Organizations typically try to solve those problems one at a time as if there is a particular sequence they need to go through. They adopt programs such as Lean and Six Sigma to simplify and control processes; they send frontline leaders to communication seminars; they might even have management retreats. Trying to solve these major problems one at a time is a recipe for failure.

It might sound like I oppose each of these solutions. I don't. What I oppose is that, taken individually, they each apply to only one area of an organization's change needs. The result is piecemeal change that doesn't last because *all* of these areas are interconnected. And through globalization, technology, greater competition, higher customer requirements, and disruptive innovations, they will become even more interconnected. Instead of one at a time, organizations need to pursue the following four goals *all at once*:

- Simplify processes
- Enhance frontline leaders' behaviors
- Simplify operational systems
- Embolden senior leaders to innovate and pursue new growth

Run-Improve-Grow takes a systemic approach to improvement. Many change initiatives typically use only one of those models in isolation, but RIG acts more like an extreme business makeover. It's not just about one particular area of the organization: it tackles the entire business, so process, systems, management, and leadership improvements are *all* undertaken and not necessarily in a rigid sequence. There will most likely be overlap as gains in one area open opportunities in other areas.

Think of it like juggling. To juggle, you don't throw the first ball in the air, set it down to pick up the second, and then throw the second ball in the air only to put it down to pick up and throw the third. As soon as the first ball is airborne, you throw the second, and very quickly after that, the third. All the balls are moving at the same time. There's no waiting. All of the balls are part of the same system.

Focusing on a single category of improvement effort is ineffective. That silo approach to change doesn't optimize. It doesn't simplify. It's limited, and it creates a false sense of progress. Expecting sustainable change from undertaking an improvement project in a single area is like trying to lose weight by only doing bicep curls. Turning such focused attention on your arms does nothing for your abdomen or legs, nor does it do much in the way of creating an overall healthy lifestyle. If you do nothing but bicep curls, you'll definitely see results, but only in your biceps. What happens after that? Do you stop doing bicep curls (because your arms are now toned) and focus on what you eat for lunch? Approaching the problem one facet at a time doesn't make sense—in health or in business.

Tripping on Deadly Behavior

Seven negative mindsets can trip up even the most vigilant organizations if they're not careful. Cynicism, negativity, unreliability,
mediocrity, apathy, flawed metrics, and misaligned rewards throw
up significant roadblocks to the transfer of momentum across
all levels of an organization. In combination, they create serious
resistance to spreading the new behaviors characteristic of Run-
Improve-Grow beyond the first department or functional area
that used RIG principles to get a quick win. Resistance blocks
momentum by impeding cross-functional innovation. Ironically,
this resistance often comes from experiences with previous change
models or quick wins that were left to die on the vine.

Those employees stuck in the sin of cynicism, who maintain an "I'll believe it when I see it" attitude, make improvement
efforts take longer. The origin of the "I'll believe it when I see it"
attitude is none other than past experience. Management appears
out of touch when an organization's front line is subjected to
failed change efforts or changes that are here today and gone in
six months. The front line may begin to believe that management
doesn't understand what the real issues are. At the very least, as
management struggles to find a change program that will make a
real and lasting difference, employees begin to doubt.

That simple phrase—"I'll believe it when I see it"—implies a
shift of responsibility to the managers leading the change and is
evidence of the deadly sin of cynicism. Employees are waiting to
see what will happen; they're not engaged to make it happen. It's
a passive but powerful form of resistance. Think of all the protest movements where police have struggled to arrest protesters
or move them in any way. Protesters (especially peaceful ones)
go limp and make their bodies dead weight. They become nearly
impossible to move *because they are doing nothing*. When employees
in organizations embrace an "I'll believe it when I see it" attitude,
it's like they're staging a sit-in protest. Individual resistance also
stems from internal petty competition among employees. (Perhaps
we should add jealousy to our list of deadly sins.) If one employee

embraces an initiative, another blocks it. Rivalries like this don't just create resistance in individuals—that resistance spills over to the group. Collective energy is spent trying to manage the rivalry, pacify riled parties, and get the person who's resisting to stop.

Protecting turf is another source of resistance. Managers especially can become very territorial about their jobs and their role in the company (their comfort zones). If they perceive changes as taking away some of their territory or stepping over into their territory, strong resistance can flare up and persist.

Related to the idea of protecting turf is clique behavior. Sometimes employees identify so strongly with a particular group at work that they resist any shift in momentum that seems to upset the order of things or threaten their inclusion in a particular group. Just as resistance occurs on the individual level, it also occurs at the department level and throughout the organization. Petty competition exists between work groups just as it does between individuals. Groups carve out territory and have turf wars, just like individuals do. And organizations are likely to have several cliques, not just one.

A unique source of resistance at the organizational level is the organization's structure and decision-making system. Reporting structures and organizational hierarchies can get in the way of progress and quick-win momentum. (Chapter 6 covers how to upgrade your management systems to support new organizational standards and behaviors.) Imagine that a work group has a great first quick win. The group took care of something simple that it had authority over. Imagine now that the next quick-win idea that fires them up is something for which they need to get approval from a top manager in another function. Depending on the organization's structure and decision-making system, approval could be simple and fast and keep the energy moving; or it could be a bureaucratic nightmare that causes a delay so significant it douses the spark from the successful quick win. When the organizational structure and decision-making system are difficult to navigate or have confusing or arbitrary mechanisms, it can create a tremendous amount of resistance to the quick-win momentum and the change process overall. Those most skilled at navigating this maze get their ideas heard and implemented. The rest get frustrated and eventually stop trying.

How Does Momentum Transfer from One Operational Area to Another?

Avoiding those roadblocks simply takes a bit of speed. If delay is our enemy, then quick action is our ally. That's the premise behind the quick win. But as important as the quick win is, what follows is equally important and even more indicative of future success. Our organizations need to achieve a never-ending series of quick wins resulting from quick action. To accomplish that, organizations need to leverage the quick wins they achieved in one work group or department across other work groups and departments and eventually across the entire organization.

Let's take a moment to examine what occurs during the course of the quick win:

- The frontline team is willing to take ownership of the new process because it's simpler and more reliable. The team is willing to increase the goals managers gave them because it has confidence in the new model.
- New interactions occur between frontline employees.
- New operating assumptions take hold.
- New roles are created.
- New management functions change as a result of those new roles.
- The huddle team highlights problems that it *assumed* were just parts of the process.

Changing Gears to Lower RPMs

Once one team, department, or division is fired up and energized by a quick win, it's time to quickly transfer that momentum. The goal is to drive transformational change across the operation, and that starts by driving it across the entire front line and continues across departments, functions, and the entire organization. In the Run-Improve-Grow system, what drives that change in vision, attitude, and momentum is a spark. At the individual level, the spark is engagement and ownership of a new function. On a team level, it is a quick win. On the frontline level, the spark can come from seeing the impact RIG practices make. In one company, a spark from operations transferred to the sales team, which requested a huddle board so it could bring visibility to quotes. The engineering function in the same company then put up a huddle board to bring visibility to design projects. Optimization moved from operations out through other functions. A team-level spark can also be a cross-functional collaboration to tackle a complex improvement project. The Run-Improve-Grow process is a spark at the organizational level. It involves making bolder promises to customers, developing bolder strategies to win new and growing markets, and having talented individuals eager to contribute and work in your organization.

Imagine your organizational energy is at the dot in the figure below[2]:

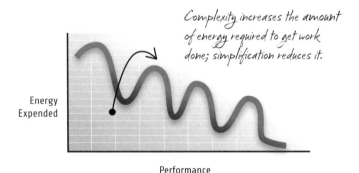

Complexity increases the amount of energy required to get work done; simplification reduces it.

Energy Expended

Performance

Figure 4.4

To get to a lower energy state and move down the energy continuum, we need some sort of spark to get us over the initial hump. Once the organization comes to a lower place of rest, there has to be another spark or catalyst to repeat the process.[3]

It takes a lot of energy to simplify enough that you rest at a new state. And consider that the more complex the operation, the more energy is expended to get less work accomplished at peak performance.

This organizational energy continuum describes the energy it takes to operate at peak performance. When you continuously provide sparks in your organization, you will see upward-trending output, not sideways-trending output. Each spark means less energy expended, which translates to greater performance because of momentum.

In the context of Run-Improve-Grow, genuine sparks are produced from interaction between mutual accountability, ownership, and engagement of all frontline employees across all Run functions:

- Accountability—having enough confidence in yourself and others that you are willing to be responsible for flawlessly executing functions where you maximize your value to the organization. Accountability is a function of ownership and engagement. Autonomy is a benefit of accountability.
- Ownership—when an individual performs because it is part of his DNA. A person who owns a function takes pride in it and persists despite any obstacles. Commitment is the essence of ownership.
- Engagement—when a person's motivation is aligned to a function's purpose. People feel engaged when their individual purpose is connected to a team's purpose. When a function is more than just "work," a person will be engaged when approaching that function.

When those three behavioral elements bond together, powerful energy is released on the front line.

To share that energy, other work groups need to develop a culture of leadership in *their* portion of the Run. Other work groups need to identify quick-win opportunities and act on them. After simplifying one operational department's Run, it's time to standardize that model across the entire operation and engage in departmental 10-80-10. Similar to developing individual confidence in a group setting through the principles of 10-80-10, departmental 10-80-10 focuses on spreading the best practices from top-performing operational units to follower units. Daily huddles need to be the new norm in multiple work groups across the entire operational Run. And across the entire operational Run, leadership transfers from managers to top performers.

Quick-win opportunities that occur in a top-performing department are not likely to be the same as quick-win opportunities in other departments. That means the top-performing department's frontline leader must model for other functional leaders the *process* for defining quick-win opportunities in their daily huddles and acting quickly on them. The principle of 10-80-10, raising the bar of excellence, quick wins, and daily huddles, needs to function like a contagion spread from one host—a top-performing individual and/or department—and positively infecting all the work groups involved in the Run. That's how you standardize *how* you execute the Run. *Standardize* does not mean making everyone the same and eliminating creativity. You wouldn't believe how many people implement those so-called standardization methods. Most end up with mediocre yet highly consistent results, and in the process they lose people's creativity. In Run-Improve-Grow, standardizing the Run is about developing new and higher standards of performance that become the new organizational norm. Best practices are shared and continuously improved.

Communicating for True Teamwork

An integral part of leveraging quick-win success and building integrated teamwork—and one of the fastest ways to transfer momentum—is encouraging cross-functional communication. Cross-functional communication is critical to removing many of the roadblocks to momentum discussed earlier in the chapter—but only when high standards are shared across the organization. Consistent high standards create an environment of greater results. At the same time, feelings of unfairness decrease, as everyone is held to the same high standard. Having high standards that are shared across the organization fosters collaboration and a shared level of performance, making these unconventional communications more valuable and effective. Employees interact with employees in other functional areas and other divisions. That gives everyone new perspectives on how and where the company can Improve and opens possibilities for sharing best practices and cross-pollinating ideas.

Once the entire operation is confident, performing at its peak, and communicating across functional lines, the next phase is to get that momentum to travel out of operations and spark integrated teamwork. Integrated teamwork is the collaboration of cross-functional, frontline teams. As we already know, quick wins spark confidence in individual frontline operations teams, so wouldn't it make sense for a group of cross-functional leaders and top performers to develop more complex quick-win projects to spark *integrated teamwork* across an entire front line?

The operations group at one original equipment manufacturer did just that when its front line imposed a new two-week lead time to win more bids. (The old standard lead time was eight weeks.) Quickly reaching the new goal of sustaining a two-week lead time would require the team to ship twice as much product as normal per week for six weeks in a row.

The team communicated its bold goal to the organization and asked, "What obstacles prevent us from achieving this vision of beating our competition in lead time to our customer?" That simple question sparked top performers from IT to jump on board to help with better information to flow the orders through the system faster. The order entry group proposed ways to simplify how orders were processed. The welders suggested methods to seamlessly set up new jobs, and salespeople began to make bold promises to customers, demonstrating their confidence in their coworkers. The momentum built like a snowball as the organization's top performers—those who had the greatest understanding of the obstacles that had been in their way—began to feel the tide change in their favor, and saw that there would be a way to remove those obstacles.

Dropping the lead time from eight weeks to two weeks in a matter of weeks prompted greater productivity, increased capacity, simplified shipping processes, and bolder promises to the company's internal customers as well as greater responsiveness for its external customers.

Momentum exponentially increases across an entire front line when employees finally realize what can be accomplished with integrated teamwork. There is a direct correlation between momentum and engagement: as a greater number of people recognize and commit to new behaviors, standards, and philosophies, more people want to get involved. They want autonomy and purpose, too, so they jump on the bandwagon.

Sparks cause the front line to change how it views itself and its role. You'll know a transformational spark has taken place when you hear cross-functional frontline teams talk in terms of "we." That shift signals a cultural shift as well, and marks the first step toward turning your front line and operations into a competitive advantage. The cross-functional front line is now looking at problems and thinking, "What will it take to…?" rather than confronting obstacles with "We can't."

Why Transferring Momentum across Functions Matters

If you have a traditional view of business, you may be wondering why cross-functional integration matters at all. Does it really matter that a beverage distributor's truck drivers interact with accounting? Does it really matter that a magazine editor interacts with the publication's marketers? Does it really matter that hospital nurses interact with lab technicians? Yes, it does. Really.

Business is a competitive sport, and those who view it as a spectator sport are destined to be left behind or even collapse. Sports analogies are prolific in business, but that's because they're apt—and useful. Any team needs to have different functions working in a synchronized fashion to achieve peak performance. A baseball team can't be full of great hitters and inept fielders. Likewise, a football team can't send eleven quarterbacks out on the field at once. And once on the field, the receivers can't do their own thing and ignore what the offensive line and quarterback are doing and when.

When organizations integrate teamwork and collaborate effectively across functions, information spreads quickly. Sparks and ideas travel quickly through organizations that have opened pathways between departments and units. Just as information and ideas travel better on a cross-functional network, so, too, do knowledge and expertise. The more connections that exist inside an organization, the better the chance that knowledge and expertise will be shared across departments and units. The level of its internal connectedness has ramifications for the organization's relevance and success in the market.

Think of cross-functional integration as enabling you to increase your degree of difficulty. In competitive gymnastics, routines are scored on how well the athlete executed the routine multiplied by the degree of difficulty for that particular routine. Simple routines executed perfectly may not score as high (let alone higher) as extremely complex routines executed extremely well. The degree of difficulty can amp up a score quickly, particularly when combined with perfect execution.

Degree of difficulty matters in business also. When your team can increase its execution *and* its degree of difficulty, think of what that does to your competition! Think of what that does for your customers! And think of what that means for your organization! Remember this diagram from the beginning of the chapter?

Function 1   Function 2   Function 3   Function 4

Figure 4.5

What do you think happens to it if you try to build on it? Imagine it's the first layer of what should be a very tall wedding cake. If you slap a second layer on that completely lopsided layer, your whole cake will be tilted and unstable. It'll look like the leaning tower of Pisa.

Just one big shift and it all implodes.

Figure 4.6

But if you drive the momentum of simplification and improvements across all frontline functions of an organization, your base layer is even—and thicker. You can add many, many more solid layers of cake (or in our case, growth) to that base.

Building on a strong, even base allows for a taller, more stable structure.

Figure 4.7

Coming at it from another direction, as your organization moves from Run through Improve and into Grow, innovation, creativity, and serendipitous idea generation are important capabilities you're going to want your *entire* frontline team to possess. Transferring momentum and raising the bar of excellence across the organization's entire front line is what you need to do to increase your degree of difficulty and execute at that new level—flawlessly.

TAKEAWAYS

- Through good preparation and design, organizations that act quickly after a quick-win success can keep the momentum going and prevent regression.
- Change projects that are too narrow in scope compromise momentum because they cause employees to become satisfied that the project is complete.
- Resistance also threatens momentum. Resistance can be from individuals or from the organization's structures, reporting mechanisms, and overall level of bureaucracy. Entrenched resistance creates stagnation.
- Companies often implement an isolated change model to Improve one area of the business without considering the effects on other parts of the business. Isolated change initiatives are not designed to create comprehensive change. Perpetual use of them does not create perpetual momentum.
- Successful quick wins result in several changes: new roles are created, new management functions change as a result of those new roles, new interactions occur between frontline employees, and new operating assumptions take hold.

(continued)

- To drive transformational change, momentum from a single department or work group transfers to other departments, work groups, units, divisions, and the organization as a whole.
- The key method for transferring momentum is the spark. Sparks are produced from the interaction between mutual accountability, ownership, and engagement, and they eventually generate the internal fire needed to power RIG.
- To transfer momentum, all the processes from chapter 3 (daily huddles, 10-80-10, quick wins) need to be applied throughout the front line and then similarly throughout the non-operational areas of the organization.
- Creating integrated teamwork is the catalyst for getting the momentum to transfer quickly throughout the organization and experiencing dramatic, or even radical, improvements.
- Integrated teamwork increases the speed with which expertise and information travel through the organization. Integration also increases opportunities for serendipitous ideas and innovation and creates a cascade effect of transformation.

Upgrade Management Systems:
A Liberated Manager Emerges

At this stage of a Run-Improve-Grow implementation, you're probably thinking things seem pretty rosy. The organization is humming. Customers are happy, productivity is up, and profits are rising. Frontline employees are energized, they are openly communicating everywhere and with everyone, and work is flowing in ways that were previously unimaginable. You may be tempted to pat yourself on the back, sit down with a cup of coffee, and relish the benefits of a complete transformation. Mission accomplished, right?

Not so fast. Even as you enjoy the positive effects of the changes happening around the organization—frontline employees taking complete responsibility of the Run and daily reactive improvements, and mid-level leaders fueling proactive improvements to support newer, bolder initiatives—you need to think of the scaffolding that supports and reinforces these new behaviors. That scaffolding is an organization's management systems. This is where most improvement efforts collapse. The management systems and processes used prior to Run-Improve-Grow will be insufficient to support enthusiastic, empowered employees. In fact, using the old scaffolding may cause your organization to revert to its old ways.

A good way to visualize the point is by thinking about dieting. Say you lose twenty-five pounds by exercising with consistent vigor for several months. You run, swim, bike, or hike, but you don't change your eating habits. If you stop exercising because you've met your goal, it won't be long before some or all of those twenty-five pounds come back, and you are right back where you started. Your system of eating was flawed even as you lost weight, so once your temporary exercise system breaks down, there is no backstop to prevent your old behaviors from destroying your progress.

But let's say that the exercise routines that helped you lose twenty-five pounds spurred you toward a greater goal, such as a marathon or a triathlon. To support such a rigorous goal, you would *have to* adhere to strict training and eating routines. You would turn your old, less-organized fitness routines into a new, more complete system tailored to your future goal, right? Doing so would make returning to your old lifestyle impossible, even unattractive, as long as you stay committed to your goal and find new purpose in maintaining a healthy lifestyle and being fit.

The process and rationale for continuously improving management systems in our organizations are very similar. After frontline employees come to own the Run and marathon managers stop running the operations, management systems need to be tailored to align those new behavioral standards. Because Run-Improve-Grow is a model that creates a *process* for perpetual improvements, your management systems will need to constantly evolve to meet your new behavioral standards and growth goals. How to do that is the topic of this chapter.

What Impact Do Misaligned Management Systems Have on Collective Behaviors?

So, we just said that management systems are tools leaders use to influence and guide people to higher performance standards. Strong management systems provide a foundation for stronger growth; weak, inconsistent, or unreliable management systems result in very unstable growth and development. (Recall the lopsided wedding cake from chapter 4.) But what *specifically* are management systems? In the language of Run-Improve-Grow, **management systems** are the structural elements designed purposefully to optimize a company's performance. To give you an understanding of how RIG defines management systems, some example systems are:

- Organizational structure—titles, organizational chart, reporting hierarchy (individuals and departments)
- Authority—roles, responsibilities, decision making
- Direction—organizational goals, team goals, function goals, individual goals
- Priorities—metrics, projects, questions asked
- Communication media—computer systems, software packages, mobile devices, etc.
- Logistics—physical location (same office, different offices, on-site with customer, on-site with supplier, open tables, cubicles), who works with whom, meetings, reports, e-mails, conference calls, agenda items, etc.
- Reward (and consequence) systems—promotions, recognition, assignments, financial incentives, base pay structure, vacation time, nonfinancial recognition, discipline leading to termination, levels of acceptable behavior, etc.
- Teams/business development units—rigid, role-based teams; flexible, function-based teams

Basically, a management system is a highway, designed and built by leaders, that directs an entire organizational population toward a higher objective.

In chapter 1, we brought up certain provisions that get added when leaders lack confidence and trust in their employees:

- Extra meetings
- Check-up e-mails
- Emergency (and interrogative) phone calls
- Detailed (often "CYA") reports

Provisions like these replace trust and confidence with some type of systematic speed limit—speed humps on your highway.

How many times have you been to a meeting that had no clear purpose or objectives? How many reports have you had to fill out, not knowing where they were going or how they were being used? How many check-up phone calls or e-mails have you received to make sure you were staying on task and on track because someone is relying on your work to begin theirs? As you're sitting through unnecessary meetings and conference calls or reading through costly reports, I'm sure you inevitably ask, "Why are we doing this? Why do I have to be here?" If meetings, reports, and conference calls aren't related to an individual's work in an energizing way, they can reinforce the dead weight of inertia that keeps the organization from moving forward.

Working within flawed management systems like these is like rowing a boat with one oar—to go straight, you have to exert twice as much energy, which ultimately tires you out and kills the boat's momentum. If you try to row only from one side, you go in a circle and end up back where you started.

Frontline momentum can only advance at the discretion of management systems. Whereas management systems that have been upgraded to reflect a front line's accountability, ownership, and engagement of the Run are a spark for organizational boldness, old and outdated management systems are like frost on a budding spring flower.

Everyone in an organization, from frontline employees to top leaders, can and should build on the momentum of a successful frontline teamwork process. It's in everyone's best interest to do so. But as illogical as it may seem, many management teams have placed an expectation of change across their front line without paying attention to changes in *their own* systems.

Until leaders focus on upgrading management systems, organizations risk experiencing an overpowering disconnect between new frontline behaviors and the outdated management system.

Failing to upgrade the organization's management systems to align with new *integrated teamwork* behaviors sends a clear message to the front line: "You did a great job in your first project as a unified frontline team, but *we* still aren't sold on the team's ability to execute flawlessly, so we're keeping our existing management systems in place just in case you backslide."

Think about the impact of outdated management systems in this way: they effectively put a pinhole in a beautiful, high-flying balloon. The air, much like employee enthusiasm, either slowly leaks out, grounding the balloon, or the balloon pops, destroying any chance of another ascent. Either way, management systems that haven't aligned to frontline peak performance behaviors have a destructive effect.

How Do You Adapt Management Systems?

Management systems can't be set to automatically update. Purposeful attention needs to be given to transforming and redesigning them because they are the part of the Improve that bridges the Run to the Grow. It's a change that shouldn't happen by default. To add the *most value* on the Run-Improve-Grow journey, management systems should evolve congruently with an organization's peak performance behaviors.

One way leaders can proactively change management systems is simply by setting up new, optimized structures that are flexible enough to adapt to the needs of everyone in the organization. Management systems have to be designed to achieve the required standards. The systems must be flexible enough to work for a diversity of people with different abilities, talents, styles, and contributions. By understanding the relationship of the people to the organization, leaders can design (and then redesign) their management systems to ensure harmony and functionality, while also influencing individuals' behaviors.

Imagine a highway that's been widened to create a carpool lane, but there aren't any signs or lines of demarcation to indicate what the new lane is for. Without an understanding of the lane's purpose, everyone would drive in the carpool lane as if it were any other lane on the highway. There's not much of a reason to create the lane, right? Extra lanes on a highway can make driving more comfortable, but without simultaneous change to the highway's driving system, driver behaviors won't change. The same is true in organizations. People at all levels need to know how to use upgraded management systems. Unless everyone has an understanding of what the new systems are like, how they function, and how to navigate them, you'll experience a dissonance that prevents progress.

Another way to proactively adapt management systems is to rout out those systems that cater to mid-tier and top managers' comfort zones and actually undermine frontline progress and prevent the actualization of the organization's vision. Comfort zones breed stagnation, which is why they're one of the main obstacles mentioned in chapter 1 as preventing RIG optimization.

In my experience implementing the Run-Improve-Grow system, management teams, especially mid-tier managers, experience discomfort when they are asked to perform tasks they have never performed before. New challenges make many mid-tier leaders uncomfortable because they are used to being the people who get things right and who know the answers. Their old, outdated management systems reflect that notion, because the possibility of getting something wrong makes them feel vulnerable and exposes their weaknesses in ways they've never seen before. When that happens, they consistently retreat to an area where they can see quick and positive results.

New systems need to encourage and support people in playing to win. You want them to detach from comfortable functions and pursue a newer, bolder direction. (That's why Run-Improve-Grow encourages the behaviors of courage and fearlessness.) And the only way for mid-tier leaders to *fully* and *confidently* trust the Run is by adapting their management systems.

Once the front line is leading the Run, management systems need to provide the infrastructure for a new culture (based on trust) to reflect those new frontline roles and responsibilities. Look around your organization. Stop for a moment to absorb all the good changes that have occurred. Then boldly share your plans to build a new culture based on new virtues and using a new leadership style.

What Does It Take to Create a New Leadership Style?

What will a new leadership style look like in this new environment of excellence? Everything from your organizational structure to your priorities and communication mechanisms will probably need to be evaluated and upgraded so that they align with the new realities on the ground. You may even have a completely different set of logistics and an entirely new way of thinking about rewards.

Because much of what comprises a management system is unique to the organization itself, there's no good way to give general how-to information on many of the elements of the system beyond tailoring them to new frontline behaviors and standards. Some things, however, are universal: priorities, communication, and rewards.

Setting New Priorities

A key part of adapting management systems is redefining priorities and therefore the questions you ask. What should employees be focusing on *now* that's different from what they focused on before? Our questions say a lot about our priorities. We ask about topics that we believe are important or confusing. The more questions we ask, the more involved we are and the more those around us can see our increased involvement.

One of the best ways to establish new priorities is by changing the questions you ask. In the Improve phase, employees need to continue to expand their thinking to come up with and act upon creative ideas and solutions. And the best tool for getting employees to think and act more broadly on a daily basis is the question. Let's start by going backward a bit and thinking about the questions a marathon manager is used to asking. Consider these two questions:

- Did you get today's scheduling report out to the team?
- What did today's scheduling report reveal to your team about our customer satisfaction in the past week?

Both questions are about today's scheduling report, but the questions are very different from each other. Can you tell?

The first requires little more than a yes or no answer, and the second is based on trust and opens the door to thoughtful discussion. The first is shortsighted, and the second has roots in the past but casts its view toward the future.

Additionally, both convey the level of trust and confidence the manager has in the employee. The first question could be interpreted as indicating a lack of confidence that the scheduling report was even sent to the team; the second question clearly assumes that the report was not only distributed, but that it also included accurate information for decision-making and planning purposes. Most importantly, the different language indicates a shift in priority. The first question is clearly focused on the Run (did the process that is supposed to be done get done?). By contrast, the second question is clearly focused on improving customer satisfaction.

Recall from our 10-80-10 discussion that top performers can often be identified through the depth and frequency of questions they ask. Specifically, top performers tend to ask solution-oriented questions. Assuming leaders can identify top performers' personal attributes through the type and tone of questions they ask, it likewise follows that frontline team members can make inferences about leadership's thoughts and feelings from the questions they themselves pose. To reset your priorities, reframe your Run-focused questions.

Do you remember being asked by your parents, "How was school today?" when you arrived home? If you have children, do you ask them a similar question? I can imagine the conversation that ensues:

"It was good."

"What did you learn?"

"I don't remember."

"What was your favorite part of school today?"

"Recess and lunch."

Each day we ask the same questions, and we get the same responses. Eventually, the kids' minimalist answers wear us down. We stop asking.

Asking Better Questions

What would happen if we changed the questions? "Who in your class did something funny today?" or "What was something good your teacher said you did today?" or "What was the most surprising thing you learned today?" Chances are strong the answers would change also.

While conducting seminars and other Run-Improve-Grow programs, I have found the most common question my audience of mid-tier and top leaders say they are asked on a daily basis is, "How is everything running today?" Varieties of this question include:

- Are we going to hit our numbers this month?
- Do you have everything you need today?
- How do shipments look?
- Are we hitting our schedule?
- Who showed up to work today? Who didn't?
- What problems are we having?
- Any customer complaints today?

The question "How is everything running today?" is a wonderful question for a marathon manager but not suitable for an RIG organization. That's because the question is phrased to keep everything and everyone laser focused only on the Run and not what the Run means to the organization. (Any answer to the question will reflect the mediocrity of the question itself.)

Questions like "How's everything running?" are very superficial even when the intentions behind the questions are sincere. Some managers ask those questions to see how they can help their team. Some ask them to gauge how reliably the organization is operating. Despite the earnestness behind Run-based questions, asking them puts the priority on running and also positions the manager to stay in the Run, taking ownership for solving problems brought to him. Not sure you believe me? Think about what happens if the answer is, "It's bad. We haven't received what we need from them, so we can't get started." What does a manager do then? Tell the team leader what to do to fix it? Take it upon himself to fix it?

Let's say that, instead of just getting product out the door, an organization's management team wants its frontline leaders to spend more time listening to their people, soliciting improvements, and then taking the initiative to drive the improvement efforts. In that situation, the question "How's everything running?" has to change. Consider these options to drive the intended frontline behaviors:

- What are the two or three improvements your team put in place this week that came out of last week's huddles?
- Which employees did you recognize for the ideas that they brought up last month and how did they respond to your recognition?
- What changes have you made to get improvements implemented more quickly?
- What items do you foresee your team bringing up as problems in the next month?
- Who on your team do you foresee being potential leaders, and how have you been working with them to develop their potential?
- What were the new What Went Well (WWW) items that seemed to echo this month? Which internal group has improved the most this month in supporting your team?

For organizations that strive to raise the bar of excellence, leaders must be committed to asking questions that spark confidence and influence peak performance behaviors.

Think about it. If you want your teams to focus on improvement but you keep asking Run-related questions, where are people likely to spend their energy? Conversely, if you're always being asked Run-related questions, you'll be sure to arm yourself with Run-related answers.

But what if, instead of asking a question like "How are our sales?" a top leader asks his mid-tier leaders, "What are next quarter's plans to upgrade the skills of the sales team?" That gentle shift in language coaches the mid-tier leaders in the direction of an improvement outcome. I'm not saying that the top leader doesn't need to know how the company's sales are tracking. He does. But by asking mid-tier leaders to report on raw numbers, the leader keeps the mid-tier leaders focused solely on financial outcomes rather than individual behaviors that directly affect improvement opportunities and future financial outcomes.

Since the RIG model demands that everyone in an organization move out of her existing comfort zone to reach organizational peak performance, questions should constantly be directing people to execute new functions at higher levels of performance. Questions should disrupt the status quo, not confirm it.

So, if questions play a role in framing an individual's comfort zone, and the RIG model works to make people uncomfortable with the status quo, then an upgraded management system should contain provisions to prevent mediocre questions based on the status quo. Organizational comfort zones should be greatly expanded to include trying new things. Or, said another way, organizations should feel very uncomfortable when they aren't playing to win but only trying to maintain the status quo.

In addition to being a tool to raise the bar of excellence, questions can be useful in function identification. To avoid any ties to the Run, management teams should only be asking questions related to Improve and Grow. Mid-tier or top leaders need to reframe questions they ask frontline employee so that they don't imply only Run involvement. Management teams should be asking frontline employees questions like these:

- What new behaviors are we seeing from our customers, and what new product innovation opportunities do we have based on the analysis of our customer visits from last month?
- Which new suppliers are we talking to about bringing in new technologies to help us open up new markets?
- How do we need to align the current structure of our sales force to support our sales growth?

Questions like those indicate the management team is focused on Improve and Grow—it's not checking up on the Run.

Focusing on MVA

Part of establishing new priorities involves focusing on most-value-added (MVA) functions. Even though we've gone over this in previous chapters, it bears mentioning again. Leaders need to examine their functions in the organization and then ask themselves:

- Do I really need to be involved in...?
- Is...really where I add the most value?
- Who is best suited to own...?
- What are my people being rewarded for doing? Should we even be doing that anymore?

One key point to remember in considering MVA is this: leaders need to *detach* from the Run, not *divorce* it. Just because my MVA is not in setting up machines doesn't mean I choose to remain oblivious to what's happening in the Run. Otherwise, the different levels of the organization could be operating in silos with individual rather than collective goals, directions, and visions—and that wouldn't be any better than before the start of Run-Improve-Grow.

Basically, whatever your role or level in the organization, you need to be a sensible leader. You can't be meddling everywhere, and you can't be out on your own doing things with absolutely no regard for how they connect to the organization's direction and priorities. When done right, MVA allows each person to exercise his best muscle toward pulling more weight in the same direction. Imagine the momentum that can be generated if all team members are doing their best and moving in the same direction! The risk of taking MVA to a negative extreme is that you adopt an arrogant attitude of "That's not my job." Perhaps worse is taking the attitude of "You're good at X, so you do it." Both negative attitudes are completely detrimental to the optimization of Run-Improve-Grow and really, neither reflects what MVA is about. In Run-Improve-Grow, MVA is about maximizing potential and leveraging individual strengths. Evolved management systems address MVA purposefully.

Simplifying Run Communications

The new leadership style should also address systems of communication, like reports, e-mails, conference calls, meetings, and so on, which are some of the most recognizable elements of management systems. We use these systems on a daily basis, so wasteful systems rob significant time and drown the motivation from our teams. Unfortunately, some organizations see these communications as sacred cows that provide a sense of order and routine and bring predictability to managers' daily lives. Layered communication systems are so ingrained in our habits that managers can't imagine what life at work would be like without them!

Earlier in the chapter (and in earlier chapters), we examined how extra systems bog us down at work. Did you notice how many, if not all, of those superfluous elements involved communication? Challenge them all and assume your new reality without any of them. Meetings, calls, e-mails, and reports are all communication systems that need to be redesigned to reflect the new status quo—the Run operating at peak performance with little or no intervention. The best way to do that is to simply ask, "Are these necessary anymore?"

If we are executing flawlessly and have confidence in our team, some reports and discussions will become unnecessary. Other discussions and reports will still be necessary. It'd be hard to imagine a company being able to survive without a profit and loss statement—some things do need to be tracked. But even those necessary discussions and reports will likely take a new shape and purpose. The key here is to determine what you really need to know to give you and your team sightlines into the business. What level of visibility do you have? What depth do you need? Once you can answer those questions, you can identify the best way to communicate to get those sightlines established.

As part of a new communication system, there must be a new standard for who communicates with whom and about what. Following successful quick-win projects that have empowered an employee-led Run, frontline leaders don't need to be involved in every Run conversation. Management systems should keep communications about the Run in the Run.

Run conversations can't creep into other areas of the organization or else the manager will be drawn back into the daily grind of the Run. In the wedding cake diagram from chapter 4, the foundation allows managers to move up into their MVA functions of Improve and Grow. Plus, when the Run stays in the Run, frontline workers have greater opportunities to develop solutions on their own. As they develop their own solutions, their feelings of ownership and responsibility over the Run increase exponentially. It's self-reinforcing.

Redefining Rewards

The final element that really must be addressed when evolving management systems to match a newly defined and highly performing Run is the organizational reward system. Who gets rewarded and recognized in your organization—firefighters or the invisible people who get the job done dependably and capably? The person who expedited a last-minute delivery from your supplier or the person who flawlessly and reliably executes every minute, including the last?

In my experience, organizations often lack the right reward systems because management teams haven't accurately defined the parameters of their reward systems. Along the same lines, management often doesn't have a solid grip on what motivates employees to want to perform at high levels. Therefore, the default is safe, unimaginative, and usually involves external rewards that make poor assumptions.

Sometimes, external motivation works. Fear and peer pressure are very effective in making short-term modifications to behavior by creating an environment of compliance. They will, however, invariably have lasting negative effects. Employees will be compliant but will be neither innovative nor willing to go the extra mile. Anxiety will dominate team interactions, ultimately creating a hierarchical environment among team peers. Still, fear from management can drive specific behavior for a period of time, and many organizations use it very effectively as a tool to accomplish specific behavior. If a leader chooses to use fear or pressure as a behavioral-altering tool, he should hire people who value consistency, predictability, structure, and hierarchy, and who believe in punitive sanctions. This works well for organizations seeking to protect the status quo.

There is definitely a place for this type of organizational system. If you are in charge of a nuclear power plant, the last thing you need is creative try-storming. If a leadership team seeks full compliance and little else, what some perceive as a militaristic executive style may be the best option for managing employees within a proven organizational and functional structure. Unless a leadership team can foster an all-new environment for creative collaboration and innovative thought—a very daunting proposition—successful management may mean maintaining the status quo, which may necessitate negative management tools.

Reconsider Money as a Motivator

Money is probably the most common element in any organization's reward system, but I'm not convinced of its complete effectiveness. I mean, will you do better work if I pay you more? It seems that many managers and companies think most people would answer yes. That's how ubiquitous money is as a behavioral-altering tool.

Many people, however, are insulted by the suggestion that the quality of their work is contingent on the pay or bonus they receive. Yet traditional reward systems remain comprised of financial incentives that reward performance in monetary terms (raises, bonuses, stock options, etc.). Indirectly, those traditional incentives are based on the premise that a person will only do his best work if he's externally motivated, particularly by money. Relying on traditional rewards produces short-term results rather than sustainable organizational growth. Rewards based solely on money don't necessarily support the behaviors of peak performance.

That's not to say that money doesn't have a role in today's workplace. Organizations must pay people fairly. But if money is the *only* motivator an organization uses, its employees will not be energized to do anything beyond the minimum. Plus, for a significant number of people, money is not the primary motivator, so their managers can appear to be—and actually may be—out of touch and disconnected from them.

Two common questions about reward systems are "What should I do to motivate employees?" and "What is the best compensation plan?" It should come as no surprise that these two questions are interconnected; a good compensation plan is a necessary and effective management tool. Compensation ensures that basic needs—like safety, food, and shelter—and some creature comforts are attainable. It can also be used to provide recognition—as with outrageous salaries that stroke the egos of professional athletes—if that's the only tool an organization has to recognize individuals.

Maslow's hierarchy of needs is a good tool to explain this. Abraham Maslow was an American psychologist who developed a theory of human motivation and behavior based on needs. His original hierarchy included five levels, starting with basic physiological needs and moving up through more metaphysical needs.

According to Maslow's theory, people can move up the heirarchy of needs only after having their needs at previous levels met.

Maslow's Hierarchy of Needs

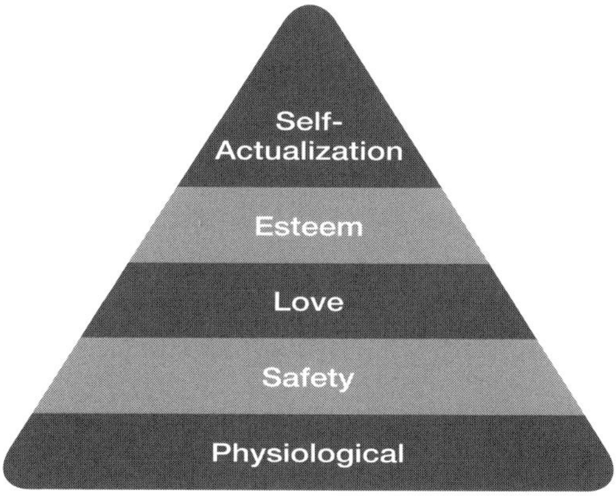

Figure 5.1

Therefore, once people's lower-order needs (physiological and safety) are met, then they begin to be motivated by the next level of unmet needs. When you look at it that way, the idea that money can fulfill someone's unmet needs for esteem or love seems absurd.

From my experiences, I can't think of a single good example of a financial reward system that has been effective at supporting team peak performance or long-term business results. Compensation must be used carefully, and it should be but one behavior-altering tool in the astute leader's tool belt.

Compensation plans are frequently designed on the premise that one individual can impact organizational goals. Too often, managers use a results-driven compensation plan to create an internal competitive environment or peer pressure. While compensation plans keyed to results can drive actions and foster hard work, they usually lead to team dysfunction and a lack of collaboration. This creates misalignment, team animosity, and frustration, and when compensation goals are not met, individuals feel cheated by the work of others. They feel that a promise was made to them, and even though they did everything they could to achieve the team goal, the actions of others kept them from realizing what was rightfully theirs. This loss is extremely disheartening and is rarely ever forgotten. Employees who feel cheated out of rightful earnings will simply not be energized to do their best work.

In one company, hourly employees worked harder and faster to achieve a promised bonus. Productivity across the organization improved, and the employees did receive higher total compensation than they had the year before. But in following years, the employees lost steam. They thought that working that hard wasn't worth the extra money, and performance was worse than before the bonus plan was instituted. In the end, money failed to move the dial in a sustainable way. At the end of the day, all that work wasn't worth it.

In the short term, there's no doubt that financial rewards trigger spurts of productivity, but that's not so in the long term. Financial rewards just aren't the reason people are inspired. Financial rewards can be one of the reasons that people join a company, and they can be one of the reasons that people don't *leave* a company, but they're not the leading reason that top performers pursue excellence.

Some people feel they have to stick around in order to receive long-term financial rewards such as stock options, vesting benefits, year-end bonuses, and so on. But if individuals aren't dedicated to excellence for their organization, the company is holding them hostage. That's a bad thing. If a person doesn't want to be there and he's only going through the motions to get some extra financial bonus at the end of a period, he can demotivate other talented top performers. That's not healthy for anyone. Basically, the compensation system based on future rewards has kept demotivated people from leaving the organization. Is that really what you want?

Tap into Higher-Level Motivation

The best reward systems are those that are aligned to individual purpose and vision. I've seen time and time again that the people who act on their motivations are the ones who get a chance to have much more autonomy, control, purpose, and value. To me, that's the quintessential motivator. If you don't have that (nonfinancial) empowerment, the financial rewards alone are not long-term motivators, as the figure below illustrates. Use financial motivators to complement those long-term motivators, so individuals feel they share in the successes they brought the organi-

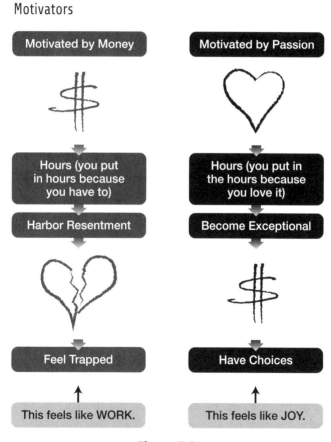

Figure 5.2

zation. Make the financial part of the equation an afterthought rather than the driver.

Instead, plug in to real motivation. What's that? Think about it: Out of everything in the world, what do you desire most? Do you seek fame and fortune? Do you want to go on an exotic vacation with your family? Do you simply want to be content with your work and to do a good job? Or do you want to be around others who are exceptional people, who are committed to a common purpose, and who are genuine, help you develop, and respect your expertise? Would you take a job with a 5 percent raise at a place where you were surrounded by a bunch of energy-sapping turkeys eight hours a day? Or would you take a 5 percent pay cut so you could be around the absolute best people in the world who inspire you to greatness nine hours a day? If you lost your job today, which new job would you take? Why? How has that changed over time?

Everyone—and I mean everyone—is driven by a set of motivations that are unique, personal, and come from within. Some people are motivated by a desire to be helpful, others are motivated by a need for personal growth, and still others are motivated by accolades and recognition. Understanding individuals' complex sets of personal motivations (commonly referred to as internal motivations) is absolutely critical when scouting and recruiting, building teams, and leading employees in any capacity.

Internal motivations change over time as a person grows and circumstances change, but, as illustrated by Maslow's hierarchy of needs, a basic set of core motivators is always present. Experts on human behavior have studied motivation *ad nauseum* and have written countless books on the subject. You may already be familiar with some of these books, but in this section, I am going to discuss the knowledge I have gained through my own years of experience, as well as share some of my own personal beliefs and strategies.

Everyone comes to work with certain goals and motivations. Take a moment and think about your own motivations. What is winning to you? How do you keep score? How do you know when you win? Why did you join the organization in the first place? Why do you stay? And do you know the answers your teammates would give to those questions?

A leader's job is to help employees understand their own

motivations and then help them remove the obstacles that prevent them from realizing their goals and fulfilling their motivations. Every leader should think of himself as a CRO—a Chief Remover of Obstacles. Too often, organizations create more obstacles than they remove. Throughout the book, you have been learning that a leader's job is to simplify, allowing employees to extinguish their frustrations and achieve their goals. In short, simplification empowers employees to feel more in control and more successful in their work—both highly inspiring factors.

The companies with the best reward systems direct them at the right behaviors, across the right time line, to the right people. For companies striving for sustainable growth, reward systems should be fair and consistent, but not necessarily identical for every individual. Effective leaders spark confidence in their employees by finding their base motivations and personalizing rewards based on what matters in each individual's life.

Everyone has base motivations that drive their thinking, priorities, and behaviors. By base motivation, I mean an individual rationale for performing an activity or function. An individual's base motivations can change for different circumstances: some for overall professional experiences, others for specific work experiences, and still others for life outside of work. The question for leaders to answer is, "How can that base motivation be aligned to personal and organizational excellence?" To start, a leader has to develop a relationship with his or her employees to truly understand what motivates them on an individual basis.

To get an understanding of what truly sparks people (you included) to peak performance, ask questions like these:

- What prompted you to take this job? How has it deviated from your expectations, for better or worse? What obstacles have prevented you from getting to the place you had imagined when you took the job? How do you feel about that?
- If you had more time to spend on activities outside of work, what would those activities be? Who would you do them

with? How do you feel when you are doing those activities? How important is that to you?

- What would your spouse, children, parents, friends, or any other close connections say about your job sentiment? How would it align with what you truly feel about the job? How would it align with what your leaders and peers think?

It's hard to determine someone's underlying motivations unless you have a trusting and safe relationship with that person. Motivations can often run deep, and people may be reluctant to divulge what drives them until they really trust you. But knowing deeply personal information—such as that a certain employee likes spending time raising his children, that another enjoys spending time with his parents or wife, or that another has a meaningful personal hobby—can aid a leader's ability to spark confidence in any and every individual through genuine empathy, understanding, and willingness to help align personal and organizational objectives.

The first step is establishing a relationship and building trust; the second step is creating a vision of how an individual can realize the goal that motivates her in the context of personal and organizational improvements; the third step is creating a reward system that caters to each individual's personal desires; the fourth step is realizing a deeply personal reward—a personal spark that reignites every day on the way to work, at work, and finally, away from work.

Would you be motivated by the opportunity to work overtime, or would it feel like an inconvenience or even a burden? So many leaders think employees love overtime and would jump at any chance to work additional hours to make more money. And that's true when people are still working to secure basic needs. However, once those basic needs are met, money becomes significantly less effective as a motivator. Therefore, a leader should select strategies and tools that align the motivations of the employee, her team, her customers, and the organization. Above all else, this requires a higher standard in both hiring and organizational design. What specific motivations does your organization fuel?

What does your team need to tap into their motivation? What motivations and personality traits make a person best for a certain position? These are simple—but important—questions to consider when making hiring decisions and building teams.

When hiring, a leader must look beyond skills and experiences and seek to understand candidates' personal motivations. For example, say an organization is seeking an employee who must perform a very specific task for a long period of time and with a high level of reliability. If a manager is wooed by a candidate with great skills but ignores the fact that the candidate is most motivated when she can think creatively, learn new skills, and keep up with other top performers, the candidate's performance in the position is doomed from the start. Conversely, consider a candidate who is taking care of children and elderly parents and just wants a reliable job with few cerebral challenges. Even if she is a manager's dream candidate, she will be miserable in a position that requires her to travel extensively and solve challenging technical problems.

Leaders must position people in ways that allow for alignment between employees' own goals and those of the team, the customer, and the company. It seems pretty basic—and it really, truly is. If you have someone on your team who is not aligned—and can't align—with the team's overarching motivations, it's in everyone's best interest to help that employee find another role within the company—or elsewhere.

Why Upgrading Management Systems Matters

This entire chapter has been making the case for upgrading your management systems to reflect the new reality of a streamlined Run captained by your front line. To support new levels of growth, your organization needs to have adequate and appropriate structures in place. This is especially true of organizations that are hoping to scale in significant ways, perhaps by going global or by introducing new products and services to new markets. It's also especially true for organizations that, through their simplification of the Run, have identified a completely new direction for their businesses. Upgrading management systems marks a shift into a leadership mentality: you're acknowledging that your front line is executing flawlessly and independently and supporting it with systems that will continue to allow it to do so.

The process aspect of RIG applies to management systems as well as to simplifying and perfecting the Run. It also applies to the systems in place to inspire employees, and should seek to identify ways to allow—and encourage—employees to feel driven by their individual internal motivators. Attaining ever-bolder levels of growth—by exploring new directions and capitalizing on new and different opportunities—requires people who love solving the most challenging problems. The new Run also requires people who are able to dynamically respond in ways that support that new, higher level of growth. Ideally, we want an environment in which employees want to volunteer their hearts, minds, and imaginations. Attaining even higher levels of growth, then, requires the management systems to be purposefully designed to support higher levels of growth, higher levels of Run functioning, and higher levels of internal motivation.

Earlier in the chapter, I alluded to the fact that your company will be constantly evolving to meet new behavioral standards and

Run-Improve-Grow Iterations

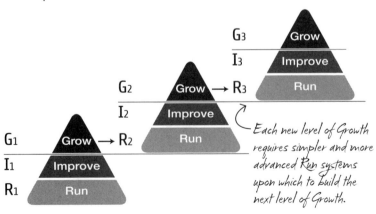

Figure 5.3

growth goals. As shown in figure 5.3, that continuous evolution can be depicted as iterations of Run-Improve-Grow.

To get from R_1 to G_1 requires a different set of management systems and assumptions than is required to get from R_1 to R_2 or even from R_2 to G_2. As the organization improves and grows, it necessarily elevates its baseline. In fact, the standards that an organization establishes to get it to G_1 become the baseline standards of a new R—R_2!

Management systems need to flex and evolve as the company evolves. If they don't, they become a straightjacket that constrains the organization's ability to grow and ultimately survive. Otherwise, the organization falls back into the sawtooth effect, bobbing up and down. Not feeling a sense of purpose or achievement about one's work is one of the greatest demotivators. On the flip side, when your management systems are aligned with the capabilities and leadership of the Run, then you are poised to focus on the Grow.

TAKEAWAYS

- As the Run evolves and changes, the management systems that support it need to be designed with purpose and adapted to support future behaviors rather than legacy problems.
- Management systems that evolve randomly are cumbersome. They cobble together disjointed, redundant activities, and that creates unnecessary complexity. Outdated management systems can kill the momentum of a newly energized front line and become major demotivators.
- Adapting management systems involves playing to win instead of playing not to lose. Managers need to make bold, calculated bets based on their confidence in their newly transformed team.

(continued)

- A key part of evolving management systems is developing relationships with everyone on the team (peers and direct reports) to align everyone for peak performance.
- A new management system should have newly defined priorities (which will be different from the priorities of the old system), different methods and channels of communication, and a system of rewards that reinforces those new priorities.
- To change priorities, managers and leaders need to ask more future- and Improve-focused questions that are based in trust and assume the work is already done—and done well.
- Financial rewards are rarely effective in sparking people. They are only one reason people join a company, and they can be one of the reasons they leave a company, but they're not the things that really get top performers to pursue excellence.

6

Fuel Proactive Improvements: A Play-to-Win Culture Emerges

With a reliable Run in place, a front line initiating improvements every day as part of their routine work habits, and redesigned management systems, you might assume you should jump right into your new Grow phase without giving another thought to Improve. But first, you need to build on the more concrete aspects of improvement and cast your view toward more forward-thinking measures.

There are two main reasons that drive people to begin using the Run-Improve-Grow system in general and to focus on making reactive improvements in particular:

- Increased complexity in their operations: they either launched a new offering, landed new customers who have higher and more complex requirements, ventured into a new market, and/or surged in volume in a short period of time.
- New leadership has higher expectations: leaders who have experienced higher standards of excellence and performance and are hired or promoted tend to see more problems than their colleagues who, over the years, have simply adapted to the environment.

Often, those situations occur together. Customers are complaining about poor delivery performance, salespeople are spending their time apologizing to customers while babysitting orders, and your finance group is showing data that margins are shrinking while inventories are ballooning. After many months of failed attempts to improve performance, new leaders are hired to solve those problems when existing leaders aren't getting the job done. Even though these new leaders often inherit problems, they are the ones who must fix them and fix them quickly. However, reacting to problems as they occur takes up tremendous amounts of time and energy—and leaves little room to develop proactive improvements that can prevent future reactive problems as you grow in complexity.

Optimized Run-Improve-Grow systems combine proactive improvements with reactive improvements. **Reactive improvement** makes the Run more reliable and predictable, and that keeps daily work simple. **Proactive improvement** fuels the new Grow initiatives by enabling the team to offer high standards and bolder promises to current and new customers. Both reactive and proactive improvements are vital to the health and relevance of an organization. There should be no compromise on either of these types of improvement. You need both.

Frontline team members must implement reactive improvements to solve the urgent problems brought on by lack of reliability. Quickly meeting these needs creates relief and buy-in among other departments and develops confidence. Once reactive improvements are part of the front line's DNA, so to speak, management can more confidently pursue bold proactive improvements through a deliberate and purposeful process.

That transition to proactive thinking energizes those who have a vision of excellence and encourages them to think creatively about the entire organization without the constraints of reacting to day-to-day problems—and doing so without compromising long-term success for short-term results. And that's what you need for the Grow. The foundation for a successful Grow phase requires you to fuel proactive improvements.

How Do Proactive Improvements Differ from Reactive Improvements?

Before you commit solidly to proactive improvement (PI), you really need to be able to distinguish *reactive* from *proactive* improvements. Reactive improvements help ensure consistent performance of current standards by solving immediate problems that are causing inconsistent Run execution. Rarely do organizations *not* have some form of a reactive improvement process. Most companies refer to that as "continuous improvement." Based on my work with organizations of all sizes, I'd say leaders estimate that, of the total time they spend on improvements, at least 95 percent is spent on the reactive kind.

The goal for you in the Improve phase is to empower the front line to make reactive improvements as they're needed so that non-frontline leaders and their staff can focus primarily on proactive improvements. To make that shift successfully, you need to understand how reactive truly differs from proactive. The difference might seem obvious at this point, but I really must emphasize that reactive and proactive improvement have distinct differences in their relationship to the Grow, their level of standards and risk, and the amount of ambiguity and uncertainty they involve.

What They Simplify

Just as reactive improvements simplify the Run through more reliable, rock-solid systems, proactive improvement simplifies the Grow by creating technologies and systems for a more predictable growth focus. Proactive improvement involves building the internal infrastructure that enables you to create innovative products and services that wow new customers in new places.

Proactive improvements in an organization function much like an interstate highway system because they are about creating an internal infrastructure that opens many pathways to growth by improving current processes, adding new capabilities, and building capacities. In essence, proactively improving how your organization functions and *expanding* its capabilities is about taking purposeful steps to set your organization up for innovation and, subsequently, growth. Proactive improvements prime the pump. They're the systems that act as a precursor to explosive or expansive growth. They set new standards in process capabilities, as well as in services offered and products sold, by raising the bar of excellence. They make what used to be "good" unacceptable and what used to be "exceptional" either poor or average. For instance, in the 1970s and '80s power windows or air conditioning in cars were luxuries, but now those features are standard. You used to be wowed by having your Amazon.com package delivered in a week with free shipping, yet now you probably experience that time as lengthy; three days used to be great, but now it, too, is considered slow and practically unacceptable. Having half of our mobile calls dropped used to be acceptable; now it's inconceivable. That mobile phone used to be as big as a brick, and today it's razor thin.

Each of those old standards resulted in operations that ran smoothly, that satisfied customers—or met their expectations—and that kept companies in business. Customers weren't clamoring for evolved services or products. So why don't we have bricks for phones and window cranks in our car doors? What changed?

Leaders' behaviors. Leaders commonly think about how they could Improve their companies and how their products and services could be designed to be even better, but the real difference comes when leaders *act* upon that thinking and form new organizational behaviors. When Amazon started in business, few imagined that receiving merchandise in the mail on a regular basis was feasible or even wanted. Why use Amazon when you could go to Wal-Mart, Toys R Us, or Barnes & Noble and come home that day with what you were looking for? Amazon's leaders, however, initiated purposeful proactive improvements. The company built the most sophisticated distribution centers in the industry and proactively increased the speed with which orders could be picked and shipped. Amazon built relationships with shipping partners to reduce time in the delivery system, and it then adopted technology that would even render shipping books obsolete—the Kindle, whose technology is more appropriate to a high-tech hardware company than an online shopping mall. Amazon pushed beyond market research and existing technology into proactive visualization about what the company could do to truly set itself apart from its competition.

To be able to accomplish crazy, fantastic innovations, your organization must envision and develop the systems *now* that will enable that innovation and growth in the *future*. That's because proactive improvements are basically the infrastructure for creating a disruptive market approach. They have a tight relationship with the Grow. Implementing them requires bold, visionary leaders who can make the preparations required to act on forward-thinking ideas and, in so doing, turn their companies into market leaders.

To position their organizations for unique growth opportunities, leaders need to use proactive improvement to set higher standards of good performance. Without these new higher standards of performance, new growth opportunities will not materialize. Your organization simply will not have developed the capabilities that allow it to easily accept and assimilate growth opportunities.

This distinction is sharp but not always visible. For example, two organizations at a similar level can function exactly the same way with exactly the same level of performance. But it's not the surface that matters. The Run might look the same, but it's the muscle beneath the surface that matters. Imagine that your current offerings are diminishing in value and there's an opportunity for the lowest-cost producer to win the entire market if it can handle all of the market's growth potential in the next three months. Are you able to scale and maintain or improve your service levels?

Some organizations—and people—view increasing standards and expectations in the pursuit of excellence as being needlessly demanding. They're wrong. Without expecting higher standards of performance and working to support employees in meeting them, organizations cannot move into proactive improvements.

Organizations that are content with the current level of performance just maintain their standards to meet current capabilities and don't strive to think about how to change their opportunities or deliver greater benefits to their customers. And as the examples at the beginning of the chapter illustrate, when you have status quo standards, you effectively lower your standards, and you'll lose in competitive situations.

When we lower the promises we make to customers, we ultimately lose business. Interestingly, the inverse is equally likely. The greater the promises, the higher the likelihood we will win business and grow. As Amazon has reduced delivery times and costs, its revenue has grown from increasing business with current customers as well as attracting the business of new customers. Proactive improvements set the stage for management to make bold promises knowing that the organization will be able to deliver.

Level of Risk

Another key difference between reactive and proactive improvements is the level of risk involved. By nature, reactive improvements are sure bets. If you Improve a broken process, you'll end up with a better, smoother process. Eliminating a redundant process or shaving seconds off a cycle time to make a product faster has success built into the improvement. In many ways, reactive improvements are risk free.

Proactive improvements, however, are inherently risky. They require transferring the fearless mind-set from the front line to other areas of the organization. They involve really stepping out into unfamiliar territories and thinking in new and likely uncomfortable directions. Because of their utter newness, proactive improvements can feel destabilizing in an environment where people have been accustomed to focusing on internal improvements that keep the organization's systems humming along and in balance. Amazon's Kindle likely felt like a destabilizing initiative in an environment originally built to receive, warehouse, and ship books. Think of all the new systems and processes Amazon had to create in order to develop, produce, test, manufacture, and commercialize the Kindle. Hardly any of them would overlap with systems in place to run a mail-order book business, which is how Amazon essentially started.

Start-ups are exceptional at proactive improvements. Because the risk of not adapting quickly is so immediate and clearly recognized by the people working in the organization (the business failing), there is greater risk in maintaining the status quo than in trying something new. However, as organizations (and people) grow and mature, fear and complacency take root. The fear many managers have causes them to play not to lose rather than play to win. They perceive they have less to gain with bold proactive bets than they have to lose by playing it safe.

Many leaders do not articulate bold enough proactive improvement targets. Without thinking big and creating a truly unique future vision, managers won't have the appetite to tackle the most challenging obstacles, people, legacy systems, or sacred cows that stand between the organization and the potential for growth. When the targets are not bold enough, obstacles limit the level of success. People try to achieve incremental goals by solving the problems within the current system rather than by creating new platforms. Bold goals, however, call for a new platform. Rarely can you achieve bold with existing systems.

Visionary change will inspire management to move the most challenging obstacles and the most sacred cows to ensure their team's success. A simple way to begin your PI journey is to create a vision for yourself. Before you can build confidence in others, you have to have confidence in yourself. One way to create this confidence and build this vision is by making sure what you envision is relevant and will help others—customers and your team. To start, make a list of all the best growth opportunities. Then make another list of your organization's chronic internal problems. Then, get creative. Create a vision of the future where you realize the growth opportunities—free from all your internal problems.

Proactive and reactive improvements differ dramatically in terms of the level of ambiguity and uncertainty. Reactive improvements are concrete, measurable, and often obvious. Proactive improvements often have none of those qualities. They're ambiguous, rarely have the same level of quantitatively measureable components, and are so forward thinking that they're only obvious in hindsight. If you are wondering whether an idea you have is more reactive or proactive, think of its level of certainty. If the path to making it happen is fairly clear, chances are you have a reactive improvement in mind. If the idea is a bit fuzzy and if the likelihood of success is highly uncertain even once you have articulated the idea in greater detail, chances are you have proactive improvement in mind. Ambiguity is a key differentiating factor between reactive and proactive improvements. Why? If the path is clear, then it's likely that the problem or opportunity is here today. You are reacting to the situation rather than anticipating it.

The timing of an improvement also has a lot to do with whether it's reactive or proactive. If your company notices an increase in Chinese-speaking customers and then sends employees to learn Chinese, that's a reactive improvement. You're responding to an existing need or exigent circumstance. If, however, your company has no current need for bilingual capabilities yet requires all employees to participate in language training *just because* it may prove useful and could open opportunities, then that's a proactive improvement. Improvement initiatives that build capabilities or improve efficiencies just for the sake of getting better are proactive. The same activity (e.g., language training) can be either reactive or proactive. It all depends on when and why the initiative is undertaken.

What Should You Expect When You're Proacting?

Expect to feel pressed for time. Organizations that know they should have some type of proactive improvement program, yet don't, blame lack of time. When many leaders examine how much time they have available to do what's required of them, there's not much left over, so they can't (or don't) justify carving into that time to work on proactive improvements. The reality is that time is a symptom rather than the real problem. Managers with so little time to devote to proactive improvements are either too involved in the Run or are so focused on reactive improvements that they struggle to move forward.

Internal Resistance

Time isn't the only obstacle to implementing a proactive improvement program. Remember, change is hard for people, and not everyone embraces new ideas and practices with the same gusto or even desire. It may also be difficult to measure success or even consistently implement proactive improvement so that proactive thinking becomes a new norm.

Expect several internal challenges when you move into proactive improvements. The status quo is saddled with an inertia that makes it difficult to move in any direction, let alone an unfamiliar one that seems more demanding. As you head into that new territory, you will likely encounter resistance and obstacles like:

- Lack of top performers in the system
- Use of only traditional financial measures
- Lack of clear growth direction
- Risk aversion
- Fear
- Lack of trust
- Lack of true teamwork
- Lack of rewards systems or ineffective rewards systems

If proactive implementation seems to be stalling in an organization, it may be necessary to take a step back and evaluate whether any of these items is the cause. Taking steps to eliminate fear and to build trust can be rewarding for the organization overall, and may spark visionaries to bring forward their ideas. Other items on the list require leadership to clarify its vision and lead with bold promises to its team as well as the company's customers.

The challenge with proactive improvement is that there is rarely a perfect platform within the organization on which to establish higher levels of performance. Additionally, the Run may still be struggling to meet today's standards and to deliver consistent performance. Between the needs of the Run and the nebulous nature of raising standards, proactive improvement overwhelms most people.

Daily customer needs generate an urgency to make things right, resulting in reactive improvements that solve external pressures on the organization. These external pressures, often in the form of customer complaints or feedback, are concrete problems that need quick responses—and most organizations are easily convinced to make these reactive improvements. Proactive improvements, however, rely on the internal motivation of top performers who have a vision of excellence and greater achievement. And even when those top performers have that vision, they often confront the major challenge of justifying to others the need for specific proactive improvement in the absence of concrete and fully defendable data. Unlike the customer complaints that fuel reactive improvements, data is generally not fully available in the traditional format to justify changing standards and increasing excellence.

Difficulty Measuring Success

A significant challenge to implementing proactive improvements is the difficulty involved in measuring their success. Not all PIs are easily measured in the way radical improvements to turnaround times can be measured—particularly when PIs aren't tied directly to tangible problems that are familiar, comfortable, and, yes, measurable. Measuring PIs is similar to trying to precisely measure the emotional connection between two people meeting for the first time. Sometimes, it feels right and you just click, but how do you measure that?

Maybe it is not *that* hard, but most organizations lack an innovation index or proactive index that measures how much impact proactive improvements have. As you begin to identify possible

PIs, also be thinking about how you might measure their impact. Are you landing new customers because of your new capabilities? Are you getting more and richer business from your existing customers? Are you attracting more highly talented applicants? Make a list of potential success indicators and continually ask yourself what has changed in your organization because of your PI initiatives.

Difficulty Getting People to Embrace New Ideas

Another significant reason organizations struggle with implementing proactive improvements is that managing PI requires a very different leadership model. Consider the following very common graphic of the diffusion process of new products and ideas. The curve shows the percentages of people who adopt a new product or idea over time. The entire population, then, is divided into five groups: innovators (2.5 percent), early adopters (13.5 percent), early majority (34 percent), late majority (34 percent), and laggards (16 percent).

Adoption

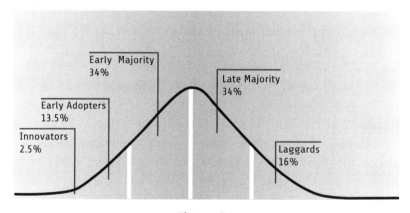

Figure 6.1

Innovators and early adopters seek out totally new products and are open to creating and discovering new ideas. The innovators were the first people to buy iPads, for example, and the early adopters were in the second wave for the first iPad. Innovators and early adopters, however, make up only 16 percent of the population! That's one out of every six people.

In his book *Crossing the Chasm*, author Geoffrey Moore highlights the gap between those groups and the early majority and the impact of that gap on the market for high-tech products. The chasm applies as much to ideas as to iPads, however, and it's even at work inside your organization. The innovative and early adopter component (16 percent) of your organization is the group who will lead proactive improvements. Those individuals will be open to new ideas, developing new skills and processes, and looking for other ways to make changes. Innovators are generally eager to try new ideas, but it is the early adopters who tend to be the opinion leaders—so if you get the early adopters, the early majority will follow. Having the early majority buy into higher levels of excellence and developing new capabilities is what you need to get that critical mass of people on board.[1] Creating an environment to encourage that support of the new, better, and different involves helping people get comfortable with new thinking.

For all of the aforementioned reasons—organizational structure, challenges measuring success, difficulty getting people to embrace new ideas—it is hard to implement proactive improvements consistently and constantly. Follow-through can be challenging in the best of circumstances, so when you're purposefully looking forward all the time, it's easy to forget to look back to make sure people are still behind you moving in the same direction.

The nature of proactive improvement means that leaders are always looking for newer and bigger opportunities for growth, so they may struggle with the tendency to move on to a second improvement without fully implementing the first. What you don't want in the PI stage is to have a bunch of fully baked but half-implemented ideas. At the same time, you don't want to be so rigidly sequential that you delay starting anything new until the project or initiative you're currently working on is complete. As with a new product-development pipeline, you need to have a few irons in the fire. However, you cannot have so many that they create a cover that ultimately smothers the flames. When you start proacting, be prepared to balance your starts and completions. But by all means, keep going!

How Do You Start Implementing Proactive Improvements?

Reactive improvements are corrective, and proactive improvements are anticipatory. It might seem simple to shift from a corrective to an anticipatory approach, but in fact it can be an unsettling transition for a company to make. And it's an equally challenging concept to grasp because it all depends on you. Just as I said at the beginning of the book, the direction a company or organization chooses to follow into the Grow is completely unique and individual to that company or organization. (I can't pick your Grow for you—only you can do that.) Even though shifting into proactive improvements is part of the Improve, which improvements a company chooses to implement will determine the shape and direction of the Grow that follows. Once you open the floodgate for creative thinking around problems that have yet to be solved, how do you decide what to tackle at all, let alone first? And how is a leader even supposed know it's time to shift from looking behind to looking ahead?

Apply 10-80-10 to Thought Leaders

The key to getting people to look ahead is to help them evolve their thinking, and to do that, you need the fervor of the early adopters to spread throughout your organization. Two Run-Improve-Grow tools that we've talked about previously can help you do this: 10-80-10 and getting comfortable with change and uncertainty.

When you use 10-80-10 to focus on your top performers and raise the bar of excellence for *performance*, you also get practice in techniques that can help you with proactive improvements.

Raising the bar of excellence produces measurable results, and in doing that, you create a slew of new data points for the early majority to evaluate. They witness the benefits and see that you have evidence to prove that higher standards produce better and faster results. Because the early majority is a group of deliberators and pragmatists, once they see the benefits of a way of doing things, many, if not most, will hop on board.

At that point, you'll have one half of your organization primed—and pulling—for proactive improvement, which is a great start. The other half, however, will directly challenge those new ideas—and they'll feel justified because proactive improvement is new and sets a higher standard without the concrete foundation of long-term market research and customer feedback.

So, in using 10-80-10 for proactive improvement, you'll want to focus on the top thinkers and innovators. Instead of trying to persuade hard-to-convince people that a new idea is great to pursue or that a new capability is important to develop, focus on those people who are willing to dive into a new opportunity, embrace it, internalize it, and almost immediately come up with a multitude of ideas for making it happen. That simple shift will change—and increase—the energy in the organization.

As you shift your attention, reassure everyone that uncertainty is part of the PI process by making it extremely clear that the outcome of PI will benefit the whole organization by generating new growth opportunities. The faster people get comfortable with uncertainty, the sharper the organization will be in the long run. When we're uncomfortable with something, we avoid it. That's the exact opposite of what you want to happen with uncertainty. You want people to be comfortable engaging uncertainty *in spite* of uncertainty.

Help everyone realize that proactive improvements are about positioning. You may not know immediately what you *will* do if, say, your entire organization becomes fluent in Chinese or Java or can reliably ship orders within three hours of receipt. What's important is what you *could* do. Having everyone in the organization speak Chinese or write code or reliably ship orders within three hours of receipt will open up opportunities that otherwise might not present themselves. Not having a completely articulated map for what you're going to do with a proactive improvement is perfectly acceptable in innovation. Proactive improvement is innovation of process—it's based on hypothesis and is only proven by trial and learning. That level of uncertainty can be unsettling to some while it's exhilarating to others.

Recognize Your Team Is Ready

At some point, however, your team will be ready to make PI part of its DNA. How will you know? A good indication that it is time to move into proactive improvement is when your employees are thinking about their processes by asking, "What if we can?" and following up that question with, "What will it take to do so?" They're the ones bringing up the fact that higher standards are possible and are setting new goals on their own. For instance, proactive improvements are already happening if employees make suggestions such as, "We don't need three days to do this; two days is plenty. That gives our customers more confidence."

Chances are that if you're thinking about moving into proactive improvements you've already seen signs of employee thoughtfulness toward processes and how they can change those processes. If you are unsure, think about these two questions:

- What behaviors are your teams now exhibiting that give you the confidence to move to proactive improvement?
- What does your daily work look like?

Review your answers with a keen eye to employees asking what it will take to implement their ideas. Typically, the conversations are already happening, and a number of top performers are now seeking your help in raising the standards. They see that the limits of their success are based on today's system. Examine how you hire, train, design, source material, bill work, and close the books—how you do everything. Clearly outline higher standards for each of those functions and then think about how you would achieve these standards with a clean-sheet approach (as if you were starting from scratch) rather than incremental changes to your current approach.

Assess the Competitive Landscape

Once you've assessed your team's readiness and done an internal review of *how* you're doing things—not just what you're doing— frankly assess how knowledgeable you are about the market and competitive landscape. Do you understand what the market is doing and who is moving in what direction? Can you offer thoughtful insights into what your customers are really striving to have or experience when they interact with your organization? Do you know which markets are growing (and why) and which are emerging, and therefore which PI will support the future Grow? Do you know what the organization of the future will need to thrive? If you don't know, you need to. The more you actively and critically analyze your markets, the more likely you'll approach your new opportunities creatively.

Even as you're steeped in the market, think about how your organization fits into that context. Ask yourself these questions:

- If I knew three years ago what I know now, what improvements would I have made along the way to make us a leader in our industry today?
- What improvements would I have prioritized three years ago to Grow?
- What opportunities would I have jumped at and worked to convert into success?

Admittedly, this is an "if I knew then what I know now" approach, but it can still be helpful in identifying the pace of change over different spans of time.

Don't get too comfortable thinking about your organization, lest you become so internally focused that you can't see the forest for the trees.

To identify ways to proactively Improve and Grow, you must

see your organization clearly in the context of the greater market and then anticipate problems (and the resultant opportunities) before they occur…hence the definition of a LEADER—the one who is first in the line.

Shift into Forward Thinking

Seeing around the corner is a unique talent, but anticipating problems and recognizing the potential for new opportunities is a skill that can be learned. It's like problem solving with nitro fuel—it gives organizations a competitive advantage because they won't have to stop to solve a crisis.

A fast and easy way to begin shifting to forward thinking is to start asking, "What if…?" Think about some of the product and service innovations we take for granted today. At some point in the past, someone asked:

- What if we didn't have to sail around South America to travel from the Atlantic Ocean to the Pacific Ocean?
- What if we could carry thousands of songs in a small device in our pocket, a device that wouldn't skip?
- What if we could correct eyesight without glasses?
- What if we could make instant coffee that tasted like fresh brewed?
- What if computers were voice activated?
- What if we could create lightweight body armor?
- What if a mobile phone could also be a camera?
- What if there was a piece of material between the car seat and the console that prevented items from dropping under the seat?

What types of "What if…?" questions could your organization ask to push it forward—way forward? Think about the products and capabilities you currently have and then go one step further. Recall all the times you thought, "Wouldn't it be great if…?" or "How cool would it be if we could…?" Let those thoughts be drivers for new forward thinking in your organization.

Another technique for shifting into forward thinking about proactive improvements is to generate a list of possible upgrades. Much of that list will come from creative thinking and extensive observation of your organization. Don't be discouraged if the first few ideas come slowly. Sometimes all it takes is a little flash to spark an idea that carries interesting possibilities—a prompt to help you begin beating the bushes for proactive improvements. Here are some examples that I've seen used to good effect:

1. Combine all of the improvements you have recently put in place and ask why you even needed to implement them. Think specifically about the problems the improvements addressed and examine underlying reasons for those problems.
2. Describe the way you want to do business five years from now.
3. Set a bold promise that will win more business.
4. Imagine that five years from now, your organization wins an industry award. What will it be for?
5. Imagine that five years from now, your organization wins an industry award. What industry will it be in?

Brainstorm around those answers and then implement changes based on the outcomes of your brainstorming. The entire organization should have a better view of proactive improvements with potential.

Teams can cover some really broad territory with "What if…?" ideas. How broad is too broad? Can you even go too broad? The answer is yes…and no. If the Mayo Clinic moved into the hotel industry, that might be too broad. But if Mayo were to implement improvements to make checking into the hospital as pleasant as checking into a Ritz-Carlton, that might be just right. You want to look for ideas all the way out to the edges of your industry—and, like that Mayo Clinic/Ritz-Carlton example shows, a bit beyond.

Think about the industry you're serving today. What companies do you consider to be part of your industry? Do you consider your suppliers as part of your industry or part of another industry? By identifying the set of companies or types of companies that make up your industry, you can start examining how those various companies do business. The educational publishing industry is made up of publishers and book packagers, the companies that actually convert ideas into manuscripts and manuscripts into books. In the past decade, the edges of the industry have changed and now include technology-only companies that have nothing to do with books, workbooks, or worksheets. Organizations that were closer to the center of the industry now find themselves competing against companies that weren't even *in* their industry ten years ago and were only outliers five years ago.

As you look to the edges of your industry, keep your eyes on the outliers who may have something to tell you about the infrastructure you'll need to build to speed past the competition, be they stalwarts or start-ups.

Beware, however. Staying focused on your own industry is the best way to fall into a mind-set of "We've always done it this way" or "That's how it's done." So, to prevent falling into that trap, you've got to look beyond your industry. Standard ideas from other industries can be earth-shattering changes in yours, like the hospital check-in example above.

Looking beyond your industry requires practicing curiosity, one of the key behaviors that helps you resist the deadly sins of apathy and mediocrity. Be interested in finding out what companies in other industries do and how they do it. The more you scan the environment for ideas, the more connections you'll see and the more ideas will germinate.

Why Proactive Improvement Matters

Despite all the struggles and challenges related to such a nebulous concept, don't shrink from proactive improvement. It's necessary for moving into strong growth because it helps management see where it can make bold promises and know that the front line is already on board to deliver.

Proactive improvement is important for achieving transformational growth and becoming a market leader. In fact, engaging in proactive improvement is one of the traits that separates market leaders from laggards. Laggards are just that—organizations that lag behind. They react to what someone else does and they finally grasp the market standard through lost sales and customer complaints. Once they realize they are failing miserably, they triage the situation and try to mimic the success of the market leader they are imitating.

Don't confuse laggards with fast followers. Today, being a fast follower can be a sound business strategy. The existence of the Internet, speed of communications, mobility of people, and other factors make the fast-follower model very effective. (Many Chinese companies have done a great job perfecting the fast-follower model.)

The proliferation of fast followers has brought an end to the era of putting something new out to market and having years to enjoy the fruits of that research and development. Because fast followers can adapt so quickly to new ideas and new standards, organizations seeking market leadership must be even more effective at proactive improvement to keep themselves continually on the cutting edge.

Not every organization is meant to be on the cutting edge of its market—some fast followers have businesses that do better than some market leaders. They have perfected the quick prototyping, marketing position, and supply chain management systems that allow them to succeed. All of these could be examples of PI. Top fast followers have systems in place to quickly adapt.

Leaders with visions of greatness and with dedicated work forces who exude creativity, leadership, and motivation should take note that there can be consequences to ignoring proactive improvements:

- Enabling mediocrity
- Accelerating talent loss (or, even worse, keeping bad talent or having good talent mentally check out)
- Commoditization of your highest-value product or service
- Slow growth

- Higher overhead
- Business decline without realizing it
- Inability to respond to a quickly evolving competitive landscape
- Loss of many business opportunities you didn't even realize were available

This final consequence is the loss of growth opportunities. The loss of opportunities is the largest loss, and it can't be accurately calculated. Without constantly working toward extensive market knowledge—and using that knowledge to assess prospective business—it is impossible to quantify how much business an organization loses by not acting. Missing out on opportunities translates into slow or no growth, but it also results in a decline in existing business. Great talent that never even considers the organization because of its mediocre reputation is a significant lost opportunity. (How many great people could have been a part of your team but didn't even consider your organization because it had no spark?

Customers and talent are looking for companies on the cutting edge and they want to work with organizations that are thinking about the future in new and unique ways. Not having a proactive improvement system in place is a sign to customers and talent that you are not positioned to be successful with new growth opportunities. That does not inspire confidence, and ultimately, it's bad for business. Lack of a PI system also hampers your ability to make bold promises, a critical link to the Grow and the topic of the next chapter.

TAKEAWAYS

- Proactive improvements set new standards in processes by raising the bar of excellence and solving problems that have never been addressed before.

(continued)

- Companies need reactive improvements to make the Run more reliable and predictable and need proactive improvements to fuel new growth.
- Proactive improvements should keep the business simple despite the complexity that comes with new growth.
- Low standards create weaknesses that cause customers to stop doing business with an organization. Higher standards inspire confidence and create customer loyalty.
- Throwing the same resources you've used in the past at a different problem does not necessarily result in higher performance. Often, the opposite is true.
- Proactive improvements are unique to each firm.
- Employees give clear signals when they're ready for proactive improvement initiatives.
- Organizations struggle with implementing proactive improvements because only 16 percent of people are eager and/or interested in quickly adopting new ideas.
- Proactive improvement is critical for moving into a strong Grow.
- Measuring the success of proactive improvement is difficult because current metrics are backward looking and data based. Proactive improvement is forward looking and harder to quantify.
- A perpetual process for proactive improvement helps organizations take control of their destinies rather than being victims of the economy or a highly competitive marketplace.

PART III

GROW

BLAZING A TRAIL FOR GROWTH

7

Make (Then Keep) Bold Promises: Confidence in Flawless Execution

Once you've got your Run locked into place (R_1) and your management systems focused on the Improve (I_1), the next step is to move into Grow mode. But how do you spark your organization to that Grow level? What gets you to G_1 to begin with?

The spark is: making and keeping bold promises. For example, Mike Neary, a builder of luxury log homes in the Pacific Northwest, embraces a philosophy of always saying yes to customer requests. When Walt Disney was planning to build its Fort Wilderness Lodge in Orlando, the company recruited four contractors who would be given a preliminary trial of 10 percent of the overall project. Time and again during discussions, the Disney architects would ask, "Can you do this? Can you do that?" Mike would reply, "Yes, we can do that." At one point, the architects asked, "Can you bend logs?" Neary said, "Sure." Even though his team had never bent logs before.

Figure 7.1

Bending logs is a pretty bold promise. Some might have said it was impossible to keep. Not Neary. Instead of responding reflexively "we can't do that and here's why," Neary's response is more representative of a culture focusing on what it will take to accomplish the most demanding requests. He and his team invented a warehouse-sized steam cabinet for logs. Logs would steam for days, and when they came out, they were like gigantic spaghetti strands that could be shaped into place. Problem solved. Bent logs shipped to Orlando. Promise fulfilled. Neary went on to win the contract to complete the construction of Disney's Wilderness Lodge.[1] Without having said yes to a demanding request—one that many contractors might have deemed impossible—Neary would not have created his next level of competitive advantage and growth.

To launch your organization up to the level of Grow, you need to make and keep bold promises, just like Mike Neary did. So, what's keeping you from doing just that?

Why Not Make Bold Promises?

If bold promises lead to innovation, and innovation is a key to long-term organizational sustainability, what prevents companies from making bold promises? Lots of things. From my experience, fear has probably been the greatest culprit—making bold promises is a risky proposition for nearly all organizations except start-ups, which have to be fearless to survive. Companies that can't rely unquestioningly on their front line are never going to be able to commit to bold actions.

One source of fear stems from past experiences with uncomfortable customer conversations. Think about it. When the Run is unreliable, companies receive a variety of customer complaints:

- The flowers were wilted.
- The server was rude.
- You lost my luggage.
- The delivery was late.
- You charged me more than you said you would.

Unreliable processes open a company up to a barrage of customer complaints and quality issues. Once that same company has solidified its Run, however, leaders may still be reluctant to make promises, fearing the organization can't deliver. They may be hesitant to make *any* promises, let alone go out on a limb with bold ones.

Another culprit that has prevented companies from making bold promises is ignorance. They are simply blind to or unaware of what their customer might want or, even more generally, of growth opportunities in their market. Additionally, tentative companies (or stagnant companies) may be unaware that other companies in their space are making bolder promises and "wowing" their customers. The stagnant company doesn't have any sense of urgency to create something new until it's too late. It reacts to what its customers ask rather than knowing what its customers really want.

Internal Focus

One common cause of that ignorance is that companies are so focused internally for performance cues that they're blind to external needs and opportunities. The world passes them by. As we've noted before, organizational objectives should be tied to customers or other *external* associations as a means of uniting everyone in the organization toward one common goal and also as a means of inspiring new products and services. Too often, organizations measure the success of their improvements or initiatives based on where they were, as opposed to the rate at which they are improving relative to the competition.

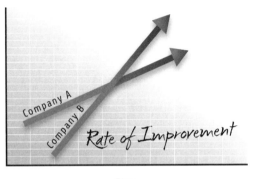

Time

Figure 7.2

Rarely is an organization worse than its own prior performance. What really matters is its rate of improvement relative to the competition. If there weren't higher customer expectations or increases in complexity, every organization would become better through continuously improving its existing system. But even if you are making lots of internal progress, you might not be making any headway against your competition. The winning organization is the one that improves the way it makes improvements. It's not whether you're improving, but the rate at which you're doing so. In a 100-meter race, every runner is making progress. However, the winner is the one who does it more quickly. The margin of victory is sometimes so close that the race is a photo finish.

A customer doesn't care how much better your organization's performance measurements are on a relative (internal) basis. It is the rate of improvement *for them* that customers care about. That's why Run-Improve-Grow is so critical for sparking customer confidence. In my experience, "wowing" customers is a matter of developing a unified and integrated frontline team. Throughout that frontline development journey we've discussed so far, the front line learns to handle complexity with confidence. During the proactive improvement process, when they're asked to create or produce something completely new, frontline teams have a process to figure out how to do it. And that makes the organization able to provide its customers solutions that no one else can.

To get a better sense of the importance of an external customer focus, imagine you're a salesperson selling computers to businesses today. You can tell all your customers how much better your current products are than the products you offered in 1995, but so what? Who cares?

What a customer is really looking for is the company that has the best technological solutions *today*, and more importantly, the one that is making the boldest promises to provide better customer solutions for tomorrow. The BlackBerry of the twenty-first century is much better than the company's Inter@ctive Pager (from 1995), but, frankly, who cares? How does the latest BlackBerry compare with other cutting-edge smartphones from Apple, Samsung, HTC, or any other new players on the market? And what about ten years from now? Will today's cutting-edge smartphone be as irrelevant then as Palm and Sony Ericsson are today?

Compromise

Probably the single largest roadblock to bold promises is compromise. Companies dilute their vision either because they lack confidence in frontline execution or because they need to make trade-offs that benefit short term needs and interests at the expense of long-term vision and goals.

Fred Smith started FedEx with confidence, and as it grew, he made sure that delivery execution didn't suffer because of his subsequent bold promises. In the Run-Improve-Grow system, we refer to confidence without compromise as the concept of **zero trade-offs**.

If Fred Smith hadn't designed a reliable and thorough overnight delivery system for his frontline employees to execute flawlessly, do you think he would have had confidence to immediately guarantee delivery and begin lobbying for industry expansion? My experience indicates most mid-tier and top leaders compromise their vision when they lack confidence in flawless frontline execution.

With a model of compromise in mind, they offer defensive arguments such as, "There wasn't enough time or money to do everything for everyone, and there aren't enough people to make improvements *and* get done what we need to get done today."

Typically, compromise is a function of three customer promises:

- Price
- Quality
- Delivery

Waste is the result of inefficiencies in the operation. Those inefficiencies put limitations on what a company can promise its customers. In that way, waste is the catalyst for compromise. I have heard many leaders say, "We can't have lowest price, highest quality, and fastest delivery. Pick two." In these leaders' minds, cost, quality, and delivery are like a marionette's strings, where pulling on one string causes a reaction in another string:

- We can have a happy customer if we get our product out faster, but our employees are already angry that they're being stretched to capacity. Let's see if we can meet somewhere in the middle.
- We can have a stronger product, but we'll have to pay for better materials, so our costs will increase. Let's wait for commodity prices to fall before we make any changes.
- We can use our short-term profits to pay out bonuses for employee morale, but then we won't have enough capital to

invest in long-term growth strategies. Let's pay our people a little bonus just to meet their expectations and then spend the rest on R&D.

Rather than eliminating the root causes of waste that cause compromise, many marathon managers maneuver around waste because they accept compromise as a *law*. The beauty of the Run-Improve-Grow system is that it sparks waste elimination that allows low price, high quality, and rapid delivery to be achieved simultaneously.

Leadership within organizations that spark a confident frontline foundation don't need to compromise. When the Run is led by frontline employees without management's involvement, and mid-tier leaders can develop game-changing internal improvements to keep the front line humming along. Top leaders can make bold promises confidently and without compromise because waste has been eliminated.

What Is the Relationship among Reliability, Quality, Bold Promises, and Organizational Success?

Quality and reliability set the stage for business relationships with zero trade-offs. Not only do they play a critical role in an organization's ability to make and keep bold promises, they are instrumental to its success. Reliability and quality are two distinct characteristics that define any business's products and services. Yet all too often, the terms are misused as synonyms instead of being used in a complementary way. What's more, reliability and quality mean different things to customers and management teams.

For customers, **quality** is the promise made regarding what the customer will receive. It can be a promise to deliver a product free from defects, or to ship orders within twenty-four hours 95 percent of the time, or to greet customers within ten seconds of them walking into the restaurant. The promise to meet the expectation of the customer is quality.

Reliability is how well you meet the promise. Quality can be anything we define but reliability is always the measure of how well expectations are met. Most people value reliability over quality because most people don't like surprises. The brain functions better when we get what we expect. Like businesses, customers dislike uncertainty. They want to be confident they'll receive exactly what they're expecting with no surprises. Look no further than Consumers Union, the publisher of *Consumer Reports*, to verify this dichotomy. The renowned product-rating agency provides metrics on reliability only—not on quality. *Consumer Reports* knows its customers will research product specifications for products they desire, but reliability is what nails down their decision.

However, changing the frame of reference from a customer's perspective to that of an organizational leader reveals an interesting dynamic between how customers view reliability and quality and how organizational leaders view reliability and quality. Generally, customers make their bets on more reliable outcomes. To the customer, quality is a calculated bet that the organization will fully deliver on the promise. To the organizational leader, however, quality is a commitment. It is a metaphorical contract with the customer that says the product will provide more benefit, ease of use, or greater relative value than the competition's. The organizational leader seeks to make a bold promise to fulfill the customer's expectation of relative value.

Cellular devices began as a means of mobile communication. Before cellular service was widespread, cellular devices were unreliable, yet cellular-device manufacturers continued to promise their products would have greater quality than their competitors' products. ("You can use this phone *anywhere*.") But delivery on those promises was anything but reliable, so consumers lacked confidence in cellular devices and primarily used landlines, which were more reliable.

But over time, companies focused more heavily on providing service for cellular devices, as those organizations realized reliability sparked consumer confidence, and consumer confidence led to growth. Organizations like Nokia, Motorola, Kyocera, and Apple provided customers with a means of communicating over multiple platforms (i.e., audio, visual, text) in addition to entertainment (i.e., music, photos, video, games, internet), but it was organizations like Verizon and AT&T that provided reliable use of those services. Who can forget Verizon's "Can you hear me now?" campaign? The mobile phone products that succeeded were the ones on more reliable networks. In short, mobile devices always had relative quality differences, but until their service providers became more reliable, customers were reluctant to abandon landlines and use cellular service as their primary telecommunications platform.

Quality is the means by which companies differentiate from competitors, but that differentiation can only be maintained by keeping reliability promises. Reliability is the realization of how well an organization has kept its promises to customers. Companies can Grow sales in the short term by promising more features, but customer loyalty and a sustainable competitive advantage are obtained only by consistently and reliably executing on each successive bold promise. The more dependable and reliable you are, the more comfortable the customer will be in making bigger bets with you. That's when you can go bolder.

Developing reliable and flawless operations is a proven benefit of Run-Improve-Grow, and that consistency is what solidifies the Run (upon which the Improve and the Grow are based). Once the Run is solid and the frontline team can reliably deliver, Grow teams can focus on offering higher-quality products that delight and, yes, amaze their customers.

Reliability and Quality Standards in the Market

Industry leaders set quality and reliability standards; everyone else follows those standards. It's the same concept as 10-80-10: follower and dragger organizations emulate top-performing organizations. Top-performing organizations must strategize to maintain their lead. Other organizations are forced to keep up with them or lose relevance.

Maintaining quality and even increasing levels of reliability isn't good enough for our organizations anymore, even if you are considered the top performer. Innovation—actually, *constant* innovation—is the driver of growth. An increase in quality is critical to "wow" new customers and keep legacy customers satisfied.

How fast could you Grow if you could say yes to every profitable opportunity that comes your way, knowing that your front line would flawlessly execute and be energized by the challenges? How wonderful it would be to know that when customers ask you for the moon, you could reply without flinching, "Yes and when shall we deliver it?" What if your entire organization could fearlessly look at even the most complex opportunities? Without confidence in flawless Run execution, companies lose opportunities that they didn't even realize *were* opportunities.

How Do Quality and Reliability Affect Relationships with Customers?

Being able to make bold promises with confidence and then deliver on your promises is a lasting and sustainable competitive advantage. It marks your organization as a brand worthy of confidence and trust. You are guaranteeing your promise through your past performance.

Now is the time to turn your inside out. Show people what you have. Take your internal strengths and match them with the best external opportunities. (It's focusing on the SO of your SWOT—strengths, weaknesses, opportunities, threats—analysis.) Whether these strengths are having the fastest new-product-development cycle, unparalleled (product) promises, best-cost supply chain, customer service, or access to critical market data, unique operational successes spark confidence to turn bold promises into an advantage in the marketplace.

Organizations with reliability problems often have troubling conversations with customers, who raise uncomfortable issues such as:

- My food was cold.
- My car won't start.
- My drink was made wrong.
- My drive-through order was missing the kids' meal toy. (Ouch!)
- I was overcharged.
- My delivery was late.
- My nurse was rude.
- You didn't finish the job.
- The workers left a mess.
- Your technicians didn't have the tools they needed.
- My people are unhappy with who you sent over.
- Why do I have to spend so much time making sure you do your job right?
- You are costing us a lot of money—get your house in order, or else!
- Everyone else is keeping their costs in line, but you keep asking for price increases without good reason. Why?
- I am asking for shorter delivery with more product options, and you're telling me you are offering a longer delivery window with fewer options.
- Why is your online ordering system so cumbersome? Why does it keep crashing?

Once an organization has delivered on bold promises, management teams and frontline salespeople can have different, friendlier, more enjoyable, forward-looking conversations with their customers. Now sales conversations can start with, "Over the past three months, we've been 100 percent on time for you, shortened our lead time with you, upgraded with new products, and helped you secure that new order with a redesigned solution for your customer. Let's talk about your business. Tell me:

- What's happening with your customers?
- Who are the new customers you're pursuing?

- What strategic initiatives are you considering since we met last quarter?
- What are your salespeople telling you about the competitive landscape?
- What positions are you seeking to fill?
- Let's update each other on the major initiatives we both were working on last time we met. Let's start with your new product rollouts. What products are selling better than your original sales projection?
- What systems are you developing to help your leaders?
- What are the new growth opportunities you envision?"

I have seen top leaders' bold promises give salespeople confidence to go out to the marketplace and say, "Yes, we can," just like Mike Neary says to his clients. Prior to using Run-Improve-Grow, a client's sales team used to waste anywhere from 40 to 60 percent of their time negotiating with their operational counterparts on their customers' orders. Six months into Run-Improve-Grow one of the company's customers asked it to open a brand new facility near Philadelphia—in ninety days! The leadership team said yes. And it actually delivered. How? The team's manager—a recovering traffic cop marathon manager—personally went to Baltimore to open the facility. An upgraded Run system allowed his team to execute flawlessly without him for months while he led the delivery of their bold promise. Without the upgraded Run, this company would never have been able to make, let alone keep, such a bold promise.

Change "I'm Sorry" to "Yes We Can"

Assume an organization's salespeople are spending anywhere from half to two-thirds of their time dealing with or thinking about internal concerns. With half of their time bogged down in firefighting, the salespeople don't have enough time to spend with their customers. Even worse, when the salespeople do connect with their customers, the conversations center on the organization's operational problems. Based on those assumptions, we can imagine ensuing apologetic conversations like this:

"I'm Sorry"

Customer: Why haven't we received our order yet? One
of your people promised we would have the materials
yesterday!

Sales: I'm terribly sorry, sir. I will find out when we will
have the order shipped as soon as I return to the plant.
Anyway, are you satisfied with the rest of our products?

Customer: Somewhat. In our last order, several parts
were missing, so we had to go find some of our own and
connect them manually. It was a waste of our time.

If, however, a sales team has confidence in its front line's execution of bold promises, the conversation with customers unfolds
very differently:

"Yes, We Can"

Customer: Thank you so much for filling our order so
quickly and delivering it early. You really didn't have to
do that; we're completely satisfied with your products.
We wish all of our suppliers were like you.

Sales: That's great to hear! I'm so happy you're satisfied.
I'll make sure to pass the compliment along to our
team. So, what are the new priorities there since we last
met? What are you working on right now?

Customer: I think we've got some real big things headed
our way. We're working on developing a new service
arm so we can help our customers install customized
products in their systems. We've always had the
capability to make customized products, but until
recently we never had a way to install them into so
many different systems.

Sales: That sounds like a great opportunity. What made
you realize that you could install customized products
into any of your customers' systems?

Customer: You know, it's funny; as we were integrating
your products into ours, we learned that with a few

minor changes, we could get your product to help us connect to virtually every system that our customers use.

Sales: Interesting. So you have to modify our product; how long does that take you? What if we made the modifications as part of our process so you could get your products out to your customer more quickly? Would you be interested at looking into developing some changes with us?

Often, "Yes we can" discussions are innovation conversations. Other times, the customer says, "You know, while I have you here, let's go meet with our advanced team who is working on something new that may need your expertise. Can you help us with…?"

"Yes we can" collaborations really spark customer confidence. "I'm sorry" apologies drown out any sparks. When you're making apologies, you're not learning information about your customer. Rather, you're supplying information in the way of excuses. That means your customer is getting a wealth of information about your organization's weaknesses and deficits. Conversations for innovation, however, occur on a basis of trust, so you can discover a lot about your customers by simply asking what's happening in their business.

So, what do you want to know about your customers today that your competition doesn't know? What do you want to know that you and your team haven't asked your customers?

Once an innovative conversation with a customer starts, there is no telling where it can go. You should capitalize on every opportunity to uncover more information about your customer, your customer's operations, and your customer's business. A few leading companies even go as far as sending their top frontline performers and managers from other functional areas out with their salespeople on customer calls. The conversations between customers and those members of your organization can produce amazing results. Skip the ropes courses or trust-building retreats. Build real teamwork with your customers by providing opportunities for many people throughout the organization to connect with customers in a meaningful way, and then together experience the successes that result.

Confident discussions with customers can turn into mutually beneficial business conversations during which leaders and salespeople uncover valuable customer information. This information is critical for the organization to be bold in its requests. But from my experience, conversations with customers are more productive when both parties have the utmost confidence in frontline flawless execution.

Why Making and Keeping Bold Promises Matters

So what if the CEO of the Oregon Log Home Company said yes to an extreme customer demand? So what if my client opened a new location 600 miles away in ninety days? How does that apply to your business? Quite simply, if you don't make and keep bold promises, your organization risks losing relevancy to your customers' ever-increasing demands. If you can't bend their logs, someone else will.

Because you've spent so much effort and energy creating a solid front line and revamping management systems to support it, not making bold promises opens the door once again to entropy—customer entropy.

Remember, we said that when you start a fire and don't keep it going, your frontline and possibly mid-tier leaders are going to experience entropy. They're going to slowly (or maybe even quickly) return to the messy habits and inefficiencies that characterized your operations before you began the change process because they've lost the spark that keeps driving them forward. That means the return of the cynical cycle, which will require even more energy to overcome a second (or third or fourth or fifth…) time.

Customers can go through the same entropy process. They get excited about a purchase just like employees get excited about quick wins that lead to accountability, ownership, and engagement. Both parties get something that they want and that they perceive has value. But, generally speaking, a customer's perception is only as good as her last interaction; therefore, it's much easier for a customer to experience entropy than for an employee.

In my experience, customers are subject to entropy when they have an expectation built into their buying experience that is not met. Only rarely is the expectation related to price. Most often, it's related to how they were made to feel. Customers like to feel special. So when you make your customers feel special, they are buying you and your organization just as much as they are buying your products or services.

Unfortunately, just one lousy experience by one single customer might force an organization to battle against customer entropy to reassert a positive, worthwhile interaction and valued experience. One lousy experience also affects your employees, who get frustrated that their reputation has been compromised. And that's why making *and keeping* bold promises is so important. It eliminates the possibility of customer entropy. When you can continue wowing the customer by making bolder and bolder promises that you *keep*, customers feel special and energized. Keeping bolder and bolder promises also fuels the organization. The energy that comes from wowing the customer over and over is validation for all the employees' discipline and preparation.

At this point, you might be asking yourself, "Well, what happens if we *don't* fulfill our bold promises? How can we promise something that we can't currently deliver?" Those are good questions that express valid concerns. If an organization makes bold promises but can't keep them, the organization loses credibility with customers. That can be worse than a customer simply having a bad buying experience. When customers experience entropy, they're more likely to try someone else's products, but they'll still be open to yours. But when customers no longer trust your organization, you and your sales team might not get the opportunity to deepen your organization's relationship with that customer.

But that shouldn't stop you from making bold promises. Companies that have failed in the past stop making bold promises and start hedging. Customers, however, see through this hedging. It doesn't instill confidence. As bad as not fulfilling a bold promise can be, the ramifications of not making bold promises at all are much more significant. You risk losing your source of innovation. Bold promises push people to be creative, and without creative innovation to offer something more, something "wow," the organization is going to quickly become commoditized or irrelevant to the customer and to the market in general. Welcome to the commodity club.

There are as many examples of those who sought differentiation but wound up commoditized or irrelevant in the business world as there are of brilliance (probably more). Think of Atari, Betamax, Service Merchandise, Blockbuster, MySpace, Palm, Research in Motion, and even the United States Postal Service. Once highly relevant organizations, they're now in the dustbin of history, or at least are teetering on the rim, because they didn't keep up with the competition and changing markets by giving their customers truly relevant products and services. They ignored or were oblivious to what the market *did* want, and then other, more innovative companies like Apple, Hulu, Facebook, Samsung, and FedEx swooped in and stole their customers. And unless those companies continue to make and keep bold promises, they, too, could risk irrelevance. When customers and the market perceive your organization as less valuable or irrelevant, revenue dries up and the company stagnates or fails.

Bold Promises Propel the Grow

Bold promises not only matter to the Grow, they propel it. Making and keeping promises is not necessarily transformational. If you promise the expected, the standard, or the conventional, and then deliver the expected, the standard, and the conventional, your organization will not generate any excitement or energy—either internally or externally. Bold promises, however, allow a company to Grow in new and different ways, to develop new capabilities (bent logs), and to perfect its legacy capabilities.

Reliable execution is the fuel that powers that excitement and energy and launches new opportunities. It also provides greater customer confidence and greater profitability because you have:

- a simple and leaner cost structure;
- predictability, which leads to higher-quality more reliable suppliers who are able to drive their costs down due to your fined-tuned operational systems; and
- simplification of work that makes scaling and application of technology easier and faster at a lower cost structure.

These competitive advantages allow you to win more business through operational excellence—top levels of reliability, cost, delivery, and service. Operational excellence allows you to Grow your legacy business and increase your profitability with few additional costs. Profits Grow at a faster rate than revenues, so you have greater room to make bold bets and investments. It offers you the capacity to make wise bets on high-impact opportunities. Let's go after the high-hanging fruit.

To crack the ceiling between Improve and Grow, then, your organization has to reach out into new and unexpected territory. Staking a claim on the tip of the Run-Improve-Grow triangle involves expanding into new geographies, creating new products and services, and tapping into new markets—and doing all of that in innovative and imaginative ways. (See figure 7.3)

Figure 7.3

Bold promises also connect the front line to future possibilities. They can see and believe that the top leaders are pulling the organization to expand, try new things, and offer innovative solutions to customers. Those promises, then, provide a new trajectory for the organization and give meaning to the change work that has percolated up from the Run. Delivering on bold promises also shifts the proportion of time and energy in the Run-Improve-Grow triangle and expands the Grow, as shown in figure 7.4.

Increased Growth

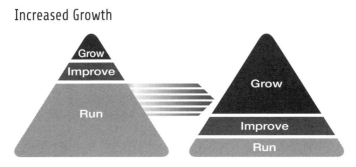

Figure 7.4

At this stage of Run-Improve-Grow, we can also envision the RIG triangle being flipped on its head, as in the figure below.

Run-Improve-Grow, Dream Stage

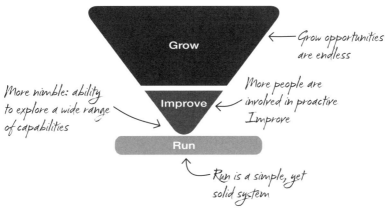

Figure 7.5

Time and energy dedicated to the Grow increase to make that aspect of the organization much deeper and much wider than it previously had been. Instead of consuming two-thirds or more of a company's resources, the Run is a thick, uniform, solid base upon which the rest of the organization can balance. And, importantly, the Run has become characterized by smoothly operating systems rather than by the number of bodies involved in making those systems operate—and by the number of fingers trying to plug holes in leaky operations. Imagine the inverted Grow and Improve as a top spinning on the smooth, solid base of the Run systems. The organization is more nimble now, so it can explore the range of possibilities across the full width of the Run and make bold promises to match.

Bold Promises Extend and Expand Your Relevance

By now, you're probably seeing the role that bold promises play in maintaining a company's relevance to its customers. Without bold promises, the organization begins to atrophy and become less useful for the customer. Making and delivering on bold promises creates a perpetual innovation spark and increases customer trust. The deeper knowledge of customers your team gains through that trusting relationship leads to customer-driven requests, which in turn become great challenges for your team. Those ideas spark innovations for that customer and enable the organization to anticipate future needs and wants.

Entrepreneurs who have turned their start-up organizations into sustainable, mature organizations illustrate the importance of relevance. They see problems without adequate solutions, feel they have a better solution, and create a business out of it. Sustained excellence and innovation aren't guaranteed, however. With proper know-how and adequate capital support, there are very few business models that cannot be copied or mimicked. And like anything that has become ubiquitous, the more people and organizations copy your business strategy, the more commoditized you become. Those entrepreneurs who understand the importance of continuous boldness are the ones who survive and flourish in the long term.

FedEx's Fred Smith is one of those businesspeople who understands the need for boldness. Smith didn't create the first shipping organization in the country. The United States Postal Service (USPS) and United Parcel Service (now UPS) were already well established before Federal Express came on the scene. Smith mimicked aspects of UPS's then–business model and made it better by introducing overnight delivery. That new service offering gave an immediate competitive advantage to Federal Express when it was launched in the early 1970s, and at the same time decreased UPS's dominance in the shipping industry. Those shipping customers who demanded overnight delivery only went with one brand: FedEx. When FedEx introduced overnight delivery, UPS didn't have any air cargo capabilities, so UPS had to scramble to stay relevant and to keep its customers confident and satisfied. Then one company allowed customers to track their own packages, so the other had to follow suit.

Through the years, there have been times when FedEx offered bold promises that UPS couldn't immediately match and times when UPS offered bold promises that FedEx couldn't match right away. Both organizations have held on to competitive advantages in shipping, administrative, and logistics areas. But the second-moving organization was always reacting to the bold promises of its first-moving competitor to stay relevant to every domestic and international customer. And that's the beauty of competition: it forces us to look one step ahead of our rivals. This breeds innovation in organizations that embrace the challenge of competition. Some days you'll be on top; other days you'll be reacting to competitors and trying to get back to a position of dominance. But long-term sustainability is about having a process to learn from your ever-changing market and to innovate where you have gaps. And that's why Run-Improve-Grow applies to every organization in every industry.

In the next chapter, we will discuss developing bold strategies based on proactive growth and the importance of spending curious time with customers, but for this discussion, the point is that without being freed to spend time analyzing customer behaviors and problems, top-line leaders fight a reactive battle against irrelevancy and commoditization. Remember the key indicator of top performers is that they are *curious*? The same is true of top-performing organizations. Relevant organizations must have a desire to explore new ideas, learn about other organizations' best practices, and flawlessly execute new functions. Relevant organizations are adept at identifying trends, behaviors, and needs that are emerging in the marketplace. Irrelevant organizations are out of balance and therefore are unable to see these trends and market shifts.

Think about the concepts of *zero trade-offs* and *relevancy* like a mind–body connection. Physical health keeps the whole body functioning, and mental health drives the behaviors and attitudes that lead to success. When there is a compromise between mental health and physical health, there is a trade-off between thriving and surviving.

Healthy organizations are those that have a unified mind–body connection, where the "physical" health of the front line and operations leads to the "mental" health of the organization through management teams' bold Improve and Grow initiatives. When mid-tier leaders' bold proactive improvements sync to the front-line teams' system and to top leaders' bold promises, then customer sparks start to fly. And just like an organization's front line can build on momentum created in a team spark, your entire organization can feed off the customer spark that comes from their extreme confidence in your entire team's ability to continuously execute on bolder and bolder promises. Your teams will start behaving like it's about beating the competition rather than beating each other.

So imagine organizationally if you were able to confidently deliver bolder promises like Gary Allen, a manager who left General Electric to become the plant manager at a small, family-held manufacturing company. When a key customer expressed serious doubts that Allen's company could deliver a highly technical product on time in the extreme volume requested, Allen offered to put the design for the product in escrow. If his team failed to make one delivery on time, the customer would be able to shop the design to Allen's competitors. Allen was committing to ramp up his operation and deliver 700 percent more product per month in less than six months. He showed his organization that the investment they made in transforming their products, operations, and management systems was worthwhile. Allen's team met the ramp-up goal and delivered 100 percent of the product on time. The customer confidence eventually resulted in a 2,500 percent increase in volume. Allen turned his frontline Run muscle into sustainable competitive advantage quickly.

How strong is your confidence in your Run? Would you be willing to bet your intellectual property and trade secrets on it? Or imagine you could deliver the impossible, like Mike Neary at the Oregon Log Home Company—his commitment to saying yes to customers is what propelled his company to even greater and more creative heights. Would you have the moxie to tell Disney you could do something you hadn't even conceived of doing before and risk losing potentially the highest-profile job of your career, let alone the rest of the work?

With a strong brand of confidence and execution, customer organizations and other external centers of influence will recognize your organization as a high-performing team. You'll start attracting the best salespeople, engineers, marketers, and leaders. I've seen it happen. It is much easier for management teams to recruit talent when their organizations have a simple system in place that sparks confidence for employees to succeed and deliver on a brand message.

Not only do Run-Improve-Grow organizations create internal sparks through the process of developing operational confidence, they also create (external) customer sparks by flawlessly delivering bold promises. Bold promises leverage internal Run system design and efforts to Improve that spark confidence in salespeople to have conversations about innovation with customers. But that's just the beginning. Those innovation conversations uncover information competitors haven't been able to acquire, and that information, in turn, provides the ante for newer, bolder bets, the focus of our next chapter.

TAKEAWAYS

- Making and delivering bold promises is critical to an organization's overall health.
- Bold promises are what propels the organization into growth, not only in revenue, but in expertise, product mix, client base, relationships, and markets. Bold promises provide a new trajectory for the organization.
- Organizations that make and deliver on bold promises create meaning for their employees and connect their frontline employees to the future possibilities for the organizations.
- Organizations fail to make bold promises for several reasons. They're afraid of being accountable for an unreliable system. They may also have an internal focus, measuring their current success against their past success and disregarding the innovation happening in the marketplace.
- When organizations are unable to simplify, they compromise and create tradeoffs. They can be reluctant to go out on a limb and make bold promises if they don't know whether they can deliver.
- Without rock-solid Run reliability in place, bold promises are costly, demotivating, and risky.
- When high levels of reliability and quality are present, the conversations organizations can have with their customers and clients change in tone and content. Instead of suppliers being defensive or needing to explain shortcomings, they enjoy the feeling of having fully satisfied customers and can make conversations proactive in nature.
- Bold promises are the foundations for bold strategies that take the organization to its second level of RIG.

8

Place (and Win) Bold Bets: Fail Fast, Then Go Big

Bold promises are most often a response to an opportunity. When faced with questions that start "Can you...?" or "Will you...?" we respond with the definitive answer "Yes." Saying yes to requests—particularly to outrageous, unusual, and never-before-tried requests—pulls us in new directions.

Does that mean we have to wait for opportunity to come to us? What if we routinely deliver excellence and execute far beyond our customers' expectations, but new, outrageous, bold opportunities don't come our way? Does that mean our ability to Grow is compromised? Or worse, is it dependent on externalities? How do we find new directions on our own? We place bold bets.

Many people liken business to a game of chess. Both require strategy. Both have players with different options for moving and action. And both require maneuvering and forethought to be successful. Unlike in chess, however, in business you don't have a complete view of the playing field. For that reason, I liken business to poker. Both involve strategy and risk, knowns and unknowns. The objective of poker is to win big pots and lose little pots. One way to win, then, is to place big bets on sure hands. Unlike promises, bets are not responsive; rather, they are intentional risks. If making and keeping bold promises is the responsive part of the Grow, placing bold bets is the purposeful part. To really catapult yourself and your organization into the Grow, you need to place—and win—bold bets on the biggest, surest opportunities.

How Do You Make Sure Bets?

Placing bold bets sounds risky. It is. And it isn't. Making *sure*, bold bets means taking calculated risks. There's risk, but they're not Powerball-type odds.

There are three main elements to making sure bets. First, you have to review past successes and failures critically. Take a dispassionate, forensic look at past experiences. Next, you need to be able to distinguish large opportunities from small ones. To really Grow, you need to capitalize on the biggest, surest opportunities. So, finally, you need to be able to identify the bets that are surest.

Review Past Successes and Failures

Taking a cold look at success and failure is a challenge. We tend to get close to our work and to think personally—and sometimes even defensively—about the behavior and performance of our team, our organization, and ourselves. To really Grow, however, we have to take a neutral look and evaluate what happened in each success and failure to influence the outcome.

This should sound somewhat familiar. It's akin to what happens at the Run level in the daily huddle when teams identify what went well (WWW) and what needs improvement (WNI). At the Grow level, we're working with more expansive projects or strategies, such as launching new products or starting up new locations, but we can still apply the same WWW and WNI techniques. We just need to push beyond the *what* to the *why*.

What Can You Learn from Grow Successes

When we examine grow successes we tend to focus on the fact that we hit incremental milestones along the project timeline, not how well we did in reaching the milestone. Because we executed, we succeeded. Succeeding without executing well happens very, very rarely and by complete chance—but there's more to it than that. Success doesn't come only because we hit milestones along our plan. A large component of that success is determined by the quality of the road map we've laid out.

A forensic review of grow success is a fairly straightforward process involving four sequential examinations in which you:

1. Review the vision
2. Review the assumptions
3. Review the project plan
4. Review the results

First, review the vision. Ask the team to identify the purpose, goals, and strategies of the project or initiative. What was the guiding vision as the team remembers it? Next, review the assumptions you made before launching the project. Identify which of those assumptions proved to be true and which proved to be false. Also identify which assumptions you still can't categorize as true *or* false. What do you still not know?

Then, review the project plan you outlined to guide the project or initiative. Examine the deadlines and identify those you met, beat, or missed. Consider the resources the project consumed. Did you use the amount that you expected, or did you consume more resources to produce the desired results? How complex was the project plan? Consider whether it had many moving parts or whether it was a fairly simple, straightforward plan.

Finally, review your results. Did the success come from the direction you expected? Were the people you *expected* to produce the results actually the ones who *did* produce the results? Find out who stood on the sideline during the project and what effect that had on the results. Consider the scope of the results. Were they good, great, or beyond your wildest dreams? Compare the results with your expectations. What changed, and was that the change you desired?

The idea behind all these questions is for you and your team to think purposefully about your successful initiatives. By analyzing the successes to see what made them successes, you are more likely to apply those understandings in future grow projects and build success upon success. That's how sustainable growth occurs.

What Are Common Causes of Grow Failure?

Failed attempts to Grow happen because of poor project design or poor execution. Sometimes, even after forensic analysis, we really don't know why initiatives fail to produce growth. They just don't. Most often, though, failure comes from either picking the wrong priorities or not executing on the right priorities.

When we fail because of flawed designs, it's often because we:

- lack knowledge of the market;
- don't understand what the team can do;
- have the wrong people on the team;
- make wrong assumptions (about markets, teams, opportunities, etc.); or
- don't understand fundamental changes unfolding in the marketplace.

When we fail because of poor execution, we often:

- didn't allocate the right resources;
- didn't meet our time line because of other priorities
- didn't meet our time line because of internal fighting and unnecessary arguments;
- launched but lacked follow-through;
- launched something suboptimal to meet a deadline;
- incurred higher costs because we didn't work to make the process practical;
- didn't follow through with phase II and III enhancements; or
- didn't react quickly enough to market feedback.

Regardless of the reason for its failure, you and your team need to look unflinchingly at your disappointing initiative to get a clean view of what happened to scuttle your success—and how to do things differently on your next attempts.

Distinguish Large Opportunities from Small

The second key element in making sure bets is being able to classify the types of opportunities that come your way. Before pouring resources into an initiative, you need to have a sense of what to expect. Think of it like planting a seed. Is what you're planting going to grow an oak or a boxwood? You need to know what you're planting up front.

The following matrix provides one way to analyze opportunities.

	PRESENT PRODUCT	NEW PRODUCT
Present Market	*I. Market penetration:* Your existing target customers buy more of your existing products and services.	*III. Product development:* You develop new products and services to meet the emerging and future needs of your existing target customers.
New Market	*II. Market development:* You introduce new customers in different market segments to your current products and services.	*IV. Diversification:* You launch a new product or service for completely new customers.

Figure 8.1

In the matrix, quadrant I (present market/present product) represents growth based on your R_1.

Present Market/Present Product	Present Market/New Product
New Market/Present Product	New Market/New Product

Figure 8.2

That is, you're refining your current system, R_1, to get more business from your existing customers. While you're experiencing growth based on better execution, you're positioning yourself to move into the other, deeper areas of growth.

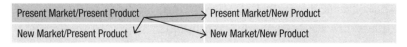

Figure 8.3

Keep in mind that you need to start at present market/present product—reaping the benefits of a rock-solid R_1—before you scale. But to fuel continuous growth, your organization needs to classify its opportunities and move toward pursuing those that fall into the quadrants that have a letter N in the label. That's how you push into new, high-growth directions; make new connections; solve new problems; and build new products, new teams, new divisions, and even new businesses!

Triage Opportunities

Moving into new territory is risky in and of itself, so identifying the surest bets in those new areas plays a critical role in the success of your new ventures. Identifying those bets involves more than licking your forefinger and sticking it in the air to see which way the wind is blowing. You need to research and gather information, critically evaluate your pipeline, focus rather than disperse your efforts, and analyze the talent you have on your bench.

A friend of mine says this about her own investing behavior: "I only invest in companies whose business models and products I understand both as an investor and as a customer." Before she buys, she researches, learns, and informs herself. On the organizational level, you need to practice the same behavior. Before placing a bet, you need information. Spend a few weeks on site at your customers' businesses. Really understand their business from multiple angles. The visit is not a questioning process but a discovery process. It's a visit based in curiosity. You are seeking to understand your customers in a way they can't articulate. A key component of innovation is solving problems people don't believe are problems. They've just become accustomed to their situation. Your job will be to uncover problems to which you can offer solutions that truly help your customer. The data and experiences you collect set the stage for identifying newer, bolder opportunities. These curiosity visits are like mining for gold. You're mining for information and data to turn into bold bets and growth plans.

Then, immerse yourself in the market. Learn everything you can about your market and similar markets. Research industry trends and analyze the competitive landscape. Go online, listen to relevant podcasts, and mine your social media and business networks for people who could answer questions you have. Talk to leaders in the market. At the same time you're gathering all this information, keep this thought rolling around your mind: What does our current pipeline of products, services, and ideas contain? Pharmaceutical companies talk about their work in terms of a pipeline. Scientists throughout these companies are researching basic compounds and studying their characteristics. Because drug development takes many years, companies need to have compounds in all stages of development (from basic research all the way through commercialization). That way, as patents expire on once-profitable drug formulations, the companies have other medicines that they can bring to the market.

What does your pipeline look like? Do you have concepts for products and services in many stages of development, so that something is always ready to break out on the market? Or are there dry pockets in your pipeline? And how do the components in your pipeline relate to the opportunities you are considering? Think critically about where in the development process all your ideas for products, services, and businesses are. Doing so will allow you to see what you already have going on in the context of your future prospects and growth.

Gathering information and analyzing your pipeline gives you a panoramic view of the possibilities. To arrive at a bet that's surer, however, you need to focus. Dispersing energy and effort across dozens of options often waters down your results. The key is to strike a balance between having all your eggs in one basket and not having enough eggs in your basket to do anything worthwhile.

The final element to making a surer bet is talent. Once your top- and mid-level leaders are no longer enmeshed in the daily

Run, they should be adopting a forward view. What talents does your Grow team possess? What talents does your Grow team need? The final chapter of the book is dedicated to this topic. For now, I'm only thinking about talent in the context of placing surer bets. In order to place confident bets, you need to have a realistic view of the talents your organization has—and of those it doesn't. Without that clearheaded view, you risk gambling the organization's resources rather than placing calculated bets on opportunities with a high likelihood of success.

To give your organization a better chance of having the talent it needs, leaders should constantly be out looking for talent assets. Scouting should be a perpetual process. Leaders should always be seeking out the best and brightest. As you scout for talent, rethink your approach. Instead of saying, "We need a marketing blah, blah, blah…" look for people who have solved problems. Ask, "Who has solved x and been energized by this kind of work?" Ask candidates, "What's your gift?" and "What problems are you best suited to solve?" As you stop looking in the same places and asking the same questions, you'll have an easier time finding people who match the new growth opportunities you want to pursue.

How Do You Capitalize on the Biggest, Surest Opportunities?

At the beginning of the chapter, I argued that the objective of poker is to win big pots and lose small pots and that winning big pots means placing large bets on sure hands. Once you've gone through your due diligence gathering information about the market landscape, examining your pipeline, taking inventory of your talent pool, and considering where you want to focus, you're ready to begin capitalizing on the biggest, surest opportunities by:

- failing fast (and small);
- shifting your thinking; and
- managing outside the drip line.

Fail Fast, Then Go Big

The directive to fail fast seems to run completely counter to my proposition that you bet on sure hands. And it might seem that I'm proposing you spend time on or go to market with half-baked ideas to gauge market reactions. Or that I'm suggesting you incorporate failure into your plan. That's not it at all.

What I mean is that you need to experiment a bit with your ideas so that you can expose problems (i.e., failures), solve them, and then refine your assumptions before investing massive resources—time, energy, and money—into them. Poke around in the ideas. In a poker tournament, when you lose small pots, you gain information about how your opponents play. These losses provide very valuable information for when you have "the nuts"—the best hand possible. You can test out strategies on small risks, so you don't lose your shirt. As you start mapping out which opportunities to pursue and how to pursue them, you need to vet them. You need to stress them. Make sure you work out all the kinks and do it fast. Don't rush into a bold bet without doing some stress tests on the idea, the process, the business model, and the product itself—on everything. Better to expose problems early. That way, you can fix them, *and then* invest heavily to go big.

Shift Your Thinking

Simply shifting your thinking from "We can't" to "What will it take to…" can change the entire perspective of your organization. The presumption changes from impossibility to possibility—and even probability. "We can't" shuts down opportunities in all quadrants of the matrix in Figure 8.1, not just the new, bold, and more risky quadrants. "We can't" is the essence of the cynical cycle and mediocrity, and it can even close off opportunities for basic growth stemming from perfecting the Run (quadrant I, present market/present product).

"What will it take to…?" is a completely different mind-set. It assumes that the new opportunity is attainable, and it positions the team for action. That's a huge advantage. With a mind-set of

"We can't," the team ends up unwittingly working against success. Having a mind-set of "What will it take to...?" allows the team to think ahead to overcome obstacles. Recall the example of Gary Allen making the bold promise to his customer to increase volume by 700 percent in a six-month period? The key to fulfilling that bold promise was a set of proactive improvements that were implemented five years before the need arose.

If you're leading a team with a "We can't" mind-set, ask team members about the obstacles they see that will prevent success. Realize that much of the "We can't" mind-set is rooted in individual anxieties about taking on additional work (regardless of whether more pay is involved). Your team might also be concerned about the organization's ability to handle many moving parts or juggle multiple and diverse initiatives. Once you know what's holding them back, you can begin to tackle the specific issues and remove obstacles that are at the source of their concerns.

Manage Outside the Drip Line

Before explaining what I mean about the drip line, think back to chapter 5, "Upgrade Management Systems." Just like retaining old management systems can be detrimental to establishing behaviors that solidify the Run, efficiently pursuing new growth from within an old management system just won't happen. It's like trying to grow a new tree in the shade of an established tree. The new tree turns out spindly and weak and never gets close to reaching the canopy.

Once the Run offers a solid foundation and you've begun implementing improvements, your organization is like a strong oak tree with deep roots. The goal now is to grow more trees, not just a bigger tree. To do that, you have to get comfortable managing outside the drip line. That is, you need to identify opportunities that fall outside the perimeter leaves of the mature tree. Think of all the opportunities you've identified as if they were acorns that your newly strong and newly healthy organization has dropped on the ground. If the acorns stay in the shade of the existing management systems, they won't grow and thrive. (They may not even survive. Some acorns get run over by lawn mowers or eaten by squirrels.)

Think of it like trying to launch a service company using the tools and systems of a manufacturing company. Or trying to increase international sales using a domestic sales model. Or expanding into a service business when your entire management system is built for selling products in a brick-and-mortar retail environment. Applying old management systems to new opportunities is a risk in itself!

As I mentioned in the previous chapter, people find comfort in reliability and consistency. When it comes to innovation and growth, however, our preferences for predictability cause us to feel internal conflict. Those deeply ingrained preferences take us in a direction exactly opposite of where we should be heading.

Of all the acorns that grow, the organization needs to determine which are the strongest and then nurture them. Don't give the same energy to all the acorns. A good friend of mine always says he'd rather do ten things great than 100 things okay. Many organizations spread themselves out over hundreds of ideas and directions because it's safer. By focusing care and attention on a handful of fragile acorns of ideas, and doing so *outside the drip line*, the best ideas have the space and resources to grow strong.

By definition, managing outside the drip line involves new ways of thinking and managing. It's conceiving of things in a completely new way. One way to manage outside the drip line is to think of Grow teams (discussed later in the chapter) as skunkworks.[1] Imagine you are starting up a new business from scratch. You can start however you want! You don't need to hold on to a single aspect of your current management system.

One sure way to get the feel of having a new enterprise inside your existing organization is to set your Grow team up in a new location. If you don't have the luxury of multiple locations or the ability to start a new space away from your current location, create a Grow room in your existing facility and have the entire Grow team relocate there. You'll be pulling them out of the physical space reserved for their function area, and that alone can open up new ways of thinking.

Another way to get outside the drip line is to have the Grow team report directly to the CEO (or creative senior leader). That removes a layer of management and communication from the growth process and makes the team accountable at the highest level. Remove preexisting incentives or compensation models and assure the team their future is secure. Measure their success based on the new information they capture each week. Provide the team funding without requiring justifications for spending it. Consider it "go learn" money. Who knows what they'll come up with!

Here are a few ideas to spark your approach with this Grow team. How about giving the team the goal of rendering your (and your competition's) business model obsolete by disrupting an entire industry. When they do, your organization will be at the very tip of new ways of doing business and engaging customers. If you're feeling really bold, try setting your Grow team up as a new entity and provide its members an avenue to ownership by guaranteeing the company will buy what the team creates. Set the team members up to be entrepreneurs within your business. By seeding multiple start-up acorns *inside* your organization, you multiply your chances for identifying and capitalizing on real growth opportunities *outside* the view of your competition in particular and the market in general.

What's Involved in Assembling Grow Teams?

Once the Run is reliably being performed by the front line, organizational leaders and top performers can focus their attention on creating a newer, bolder road map. But there's more to developing a new road map than just setting leaders and top performers free to strategize. Placing bold bets—then playing to win them—requires working in Grow teams and collaborating with customers and suppliers.

Drafting the Right Players

Your automatic assumption is probably that the Grow team is a variation of your senior leadership. Not necessarily. **Grow teams** consist of top performers (who can be in management roles but don't have to be) in multiple areas who are assigned the responsibility of placing bold bets and developing plans to win them.[2]

Look at your talent pool. Who has been able to create something from nothing? Who are the entrepreneurs inside the organization? Identify those people and recruit them to be on your Grow team. Any bet, even a sure one, brings with it a level of uncertainty, so find people who are comfortable with ambiguity and are able to work on assumptions rather than those who need certainty. For that reason, you also want to identify and invite fearless people to be on the Grow team. Going into new and unfamiliar territory takes courage, and you need a Grow team composed of people who are fearless and determined. You want people whose default position when confronting obstacles is, "What will it take to…?" rather than people whose default is, "We can't."

Grow team members should also be top performers who have innovative minds and have shown they can initiate without being asked. When members share those characteristics, they feed off one another to promote the most vivid and creative ideas for the organization to pursue.

A Grow team's members should have demonstrated the ability to see new potential rather than maintain status quo, and the team could include representatives from every area, including:

- Sales
- Finance
- Technology
- Marketing
- Accounting
- Supply chain
- Operations
- Past employees

- Current customers
- Past customers
- Key suppliers
- Market experts

Diverse representation in a Grow team is critical for generating a broad range of innovative ideas, not to mention that you need people with various capabilities to turn those ideas into reality! Once an innovative vision has been established, together the various departments and functions can confidently piece together the steps required to execute a bold road map.

Recognizing When You Have a Good Team

Just because you've assembled a Grow team doesn't mean it'll be a good Grow team. The best Grow teams share certain qualities, and likewise, there are definite characteristics you should look out for as signs that your Grow team will ultimately be unsuccessful.
The best Grow teams:

- are made up of a few individuals who possess good knowledge of the entire system, not just of their function in it;
- seek solutions to problems rather than identify reasons that proposed solutions won't work;
- seek collaboration with "ANDs" (instead of "ORs") by building on each other's ideas;
- have members who truly respect and trust one another for their previous successes in breaking through obstacles;
- scrutinize ideas and dig into the fine details instead of jump at the first idea;
- seek to understand the *why* behind something rather than just the *what*; and
- seek to add other talents and skills to their team rather than believe they know it all.

By contrast, the unsuccessful Grow teams I've seen are those that compromise on a direction because it is convenient to the interests of individuals. Members bicker over the wrong problems—mostly internal politics—rather than debating where the marketplace is going. Individual members seek personal recognition rather than a team win. They waste time insisting those who have a vision prove everything with data rather than go with some assumptions for the sake of innovation. Rather than see the possibilities first and make a plan to reach them, unsuccessful Grow teams limit their vision based first on how much work they personally have to do. In the end, Grow teams fail due to lack of inspiration—unsuccessful Grow teams lack vision, team confidence, and the perspective of "what will it take."

Clarifying the Grow Team's Role in Making Bold Bets

It's simple to describe a Grow team and outline all its functions, but what does a Grow team really *do*? Recently, one of Ron Stibich's Grow teams at Evercoat went through the innovation study process to develop a new solution for automotive and marine markets that eliminated the use of finishing putty prior to paint application. Multiple Grow teams investigated the production processes at body shops, boat detailers, paint shops, and other similar end users to understand what areas of their processes could use an innovative technology. As I spent time with Stibich, he recalled the process of developing a revolutionary finishing putty, an innovation spark[3] for the body repair business:

> We went into body shops and identified pinholes as being a big problem. The repairmen had to stop the process multiple times to repair the pinholes they found in the putty they were laying down. And we focused on the reasons why. We found out—and it was a surprise to us—that the painter often was the person who fixed it, or he would load up on primer that was hugely expensive to try and cover up some of the pinholes.
>
> The body shops also had problems with rust-proofing materials, they had a problem repairing plastic materials, and they had a problem with the plastic that they used to mask the car.

Through surveys that we then conducted, we asked, on a scale of 1 to 10, how much value would it add if we:

- *Decreased the problem of pinholing?*
- *Increased the efficiency of repair on doors?*
- *Improved the ability to manage OEM bumper textures?*
- *Could make the product sand easier or quicker?*

We knew we had the technology, capability, and resources to make putty that would sand easier, but in the eyes of the user, that would only have been an incremental improvement. Even though we could make the world's best [putty], and the difference [between our product and our competitor's product] was significant, users didn't value that difference, so it wasn't worth our resources to come up with a new product.

But as part of our Satisfaction Gap Survey, we were told a product that could stop pinholing would be huge because [the customers said], "I have pinholes on every job, with no solution to avoid pinholing." That [satisfaction] gap was much greater. So we went through that whole process and identified the biggest opportunities for the particular market segments that we were looking at. Once we knew what we wanted, we asked our Grow team, "How do we innovate that?"

The role of your Grow team, then, is to be the organization's converter. It starts by dreaming big, then gathering information from customers and the market to uncover potential growth opportunities. Next, it has to convert. It's a Grow team's responsibility to place bold bets on those opportunities by developing bold road maps to make them happen.

It comes down to organizing the information and laying it out clearly so that it directs the new iteration of the RIG journey. The layout should have the following components:

- New objectives
- New goals
- New strategies

- New milestones
- New talent

Start with objectives. Identify what you are trying to accomplish, what you want customers to take away from their interactions with your organization. Then set goals to achieve those objectives. In my experience, too many organizations develop tactics without an adequate understanding of their objectives and goals. Organizations that tailor their objectives to their strategies end up being too tactical. Without an understanding of purpose, top performers tend to get lost on tactical journeys. When you think of it this way, it's intuitive: before you can reasonably plan how to do something, you have to know what you're doing and why—like creating a special putty to solve pinholing.

With an understanding of objectives, goals, and strategies, you can identify the milestones that will indicate the organization is moving on the right track. This is the tactical part of making sure everything happens that needs to happen to place and win the bold bet. To overcome specific problems however, you may need the skills of new talent. How to scout for it is the topic of the next chapter.

Why Placing Big, Sure Bets Matters

To survive and thrive in business in today's markets, RIG organizations need to be able to pivot from their internal culture transformation based on execution to an external transformation based on innovation and relevance. Organizations that don't innovate or scale are quickly lapped by those that do. Even organizations that execute perfectly based on aging standards of performance soon find that perfection of an old metric puts them on the fast track to irrelevance.

Relevance and Survival

Growth requires staying relevant to the market—whatever that market is for your organization. If customers don't see your offerings as relevant, if you can't even make it into the decision set, you're bound to wither. It might not happen overnight, but when you're not considered relevant, withering will definitely happen over time. So placing big, sure bets matters to your organization's long-term survival and sustainability as well.

Similarly, placing and winning the biggest, surest bets plays a role in your organization's financial strength. You have a more focused and deliberate use of resources. Instead of dribbling resources on every seemingly interesting idea or opportunity that comes your way, you have a process for vetting possibilities and investing in the best, most promising ones. It might seem like an oxymoron to suggest you invest in bold, sure things as a way to increase growth and increase your organization's financial strength. Can a sure thing be bold at the same time? It can. Think about iPhones and iPads, Swiffer, and Chipotle. Those might be extreme, but they weren't random gambles on fly-by-night ideas. They were calculated bets by Apple, Procter & Gamble, and McDonald's on bold opportunities, and each bet increased the financial strength of its organization.

Organizational Health and Purpose

Placing bets on the biggest and surest opportunities is the essence of relevance. Converting those bets into success is the essence of growth and organizational transformation. By that I mean that beyond boosting metrics related to financial strength and market values, making bold, sure bets matters for the health of the overall organization. Engagement, purpose, and the culture all benefit from going after bold possibilities and making them a reality.

Bold bets that become bold road maps to new growth stimulate most everyone in the organization, especially top performers. New opportunities create a new medium through which the excitement and confidence of top performers can continue to expand. True to 10-80-10, the drive of top performers inspires the rest of the organization to push its limits as well. Plus, top performers find themselves gravitating toward the new roles that best suit them. And as you open more opportunities, you may find you have more top performers than you originally thought, as new needs and demands reveal the strengths of others in the organization.

Externally, customers, suppliers, and new talent are also engaged in this race to the top. Customers get a sneak peak at what's coming their way. They know that you and your organization are working to solve their problems. They notice—and likely admire—the energy emanating from your organization. Your relevance increases and so does your customers' confidence. When the day arrives that you can offer your customers something no one else in the marketplace has offered (or even thought to offer), the response is simply, "Wow!"

Bolder bets and road maps also give your organization an opportunity to align with your existing suppliers—and potentially new and better suppliers—under a common language with common objectives. Organizations that share their road maps with their suppliers essentially take a mechanic, tire shop, gas station, and tow truck with them on their Run-Improve-Grow journey. In essence, incorporating suppliers into the new road map built around bold bets enables your organization to spread your Run-Improve-Grow experience to your supplier organizations. The benefits to your organization are significant. You have lower costs, increased predictability, and new opportunities for collaborating on bold initiatives with partners you trust.

The key ingredient in that engagement is purpose. People engage with others, with ideas, and with organizations when they find meaning and purpose in them. Particularly for top performers, there's nothing more draining than getting into a rut of the same old routine. That's because the best of the top performers crave opportunities for growth themselves. They want to try, learn, and master new skills, techniques, and technologies. When you place bold bets and map plans to win them, you give those top performers—and the rest of your organization—fuel to Grow. Their growth creates a ripple effect across the organization.

And that has implications for the overall culture of the organization. At the risk of sounding over the top, the culture created from making and winning bold bets is a positive, inspiring, energetic culture. It has a tempo. It's one that people really do dream of working in. It's magnetic. That kind of culture attracts talented employees as well as talented suppliers and innovative customers. Birds of a feather do flock together. Grow new trees where those birds can nest.

TAKEAWAYS

- To Grow, organizations need to place bold bets and win them.
- Placing bets on the surest opportunities requires analyzing your organization's past successes and failures and focusing on the *why* more than on the *what*. Understand *why* something succeeded or failed, not just *that* it succeeded or failed.
- Not all opportunities are equal—distinguish large opportunities from small and then pursue the biggest, surest ones.
- Growth from increasing sales of existing products to current customers is really growth related to Run maximization. It's growth, but it's not the game-changing growth that comes from expanding into new markets with new products.
- Capitalizing on big opportunities requires taking small risks early in the process so you can learn. It also requires shifting your thinking from identifying reasons you can't do something to identifying what it will take to do it.
- Establish and lead internal teams as if they were independent start-ups—you'll unleash a tremendous amount of creativity and employee commitment to growth initiatives and to the organization as a whole.

- Grow teams are created when companies put together an autonomous group of individuals representing all organizational functions and give them the freedom and resources to dream big.
- Placing big bets on big opportunities is how companies launch growth to a previously unexperienced level. Attaining this level is critical to the organization's relevance and survival and its overall health and sense of purpose.

9

Scout (Then Place) Talent:
Building Your Grow Team

If you truly believe your people are your most valuable asset and that talent drives your organization's peak performance, then to be a top-performing organization, you need to be a talent magnet. With a bold road map in place, and after establishing a brand of confidence and execution through an initial Run-Improve-Grow journey, your organization can take the new, bold road map to market and confidently say, "This is where we're going. Who wants to be a part of something great?" Developing a brand of confidence, execution, and bold innovation is the way that talent magnets build a talent fleet.

So what exactly is a talent fleet and how can it support your Grow team and R_2? A talent fleet is a group of capable individuals working as a single unit to create an incredible force of innovation and relevance. Being a talent fleet has two components. The first involves *attracting* the best, brightest, and naturally talented individuals into an organization. The second involves *keeping* talented individuals in your organization and performing at their peak. The difference between success and stagnation depends on your organization's ability to both attract the best talent and keep them inspired.

Why Do You Need a Talent Fleet?

Without growth, organizations struggle to add talented people. Without more talented people, managers have to limit what can be done. When managers can't delegate, they can get stuck in the Run or working on improvements that limit their ability to lead or Grow. Without innovation and growth, organizations don't have capital to invest in the future. And without the ability to invest in new, bold road maps, the cycle continues.

This downward cycle is most prevalent during challenging economic times, when companies are pressured to cut expenses to maintain a certain level of profitability. Layoffs and loss of talent are examples of "improvement projects" undertaken to maintain profitability. With fewer people, innovation can become an afterthought rather than a focus, yet rough economic times demand even greater innovation than stable periods. Therefore, it's critical that organizations practice innovation behaviors on a continuous basis and not just as reactions to the competition or as a survival mechanism during times of crisis.

Continuing success using Run-Improve-Grow ties back to a core theme of this book—that is, to behaviors. Communication, or I should say miscommunication, is what typically causes top performers to feel stifled, frustrated, and lost during the transition when the newly transformed RIG organization is beginning to leverage RIG to explore newer, bolder opportunities. Creating and communicating a new, bold road map is a simple way to squash such feelings.

How Do You Assemble a Talent Fleet?

Attracting talent can be less difficult for world-class organizations because they set the industry standard for innovation and boldness. As a result, people and organizations vie for positions in and partnerships with the company. Remember, when an organization has a reputation for raising the bar of excellence, more people want to be a part of it. To assemble a talent fleet, you've got to up your game, identify what you need, and scout for specific skills and complementary talents.

Up Your Game

No one wants to be drafted into a losing organization. Think of any sports team that has been considered a dynasty. What made it a dynasty was its ability to attract and retain the best talent. Even though sports is perhaps an over-used business metaphor, I like it for Run-Improve-Grow because, like athletes and sports teams, our organizations are constantly battling irrelevance and engaging in fierce competition to attract the boldest and most talented players. In both sports and in our organizations, winning is the only option when you want to build a talent fleet. If you don't think a business can create a dynasty, look no further than the fashion industry, where houses like Chanel and Yves Saint Laurent continue to Grow and innovate well after the death of the founder. Those fashion companies, and many others like them, create, sustain, and Grow dynasties in an industry characterized as much by innovation as by commoditization.

In my experience watching sports and implementing the Run-Improve-Grow system, I've seen organizations that win attract a fleet of talent and organizations that lose become irrelevant to talented individuals, who seek to be traded or retire early. The former typically wins championships year after year; the latter repeatedly drafts one of the first ten talents and yet fails to convert those individual talents into organizational success.

As I mentioned earlier, top performers always want to win, so they join the organizations that provide an opportunity for success. Talented individuals like to know that they are going to be a part of greatness; they look for more than just stability and a paycheck. Winning reinforces a talented top performer's desires and development up the hierarchy of needs.

Luckily, our professional organizations have more options to attract bold people than do sports franchises. Of course, both groups engage in talent acquisition and talent recruitment: sports leagues even create developmental leagues for their up-and-comers to get them ready for the majors. Professional sports teams of all kinds know the value of talent. Why doesn't business? Whether an organization needs a few key talents or a partnership or acquisition, scouting is critical. Athletic organizations constantly scout for the best players, but they only have one chance a year to draft them. In our professional league (business), scouting and hiring can occur daily.

By leveraging management and leadership functions, talented leaders accelerate an organization's learning curve—its speed—by empowering top performers to a new standard of excellence through the principle of 10-80-10. And as leaders are liberated by their top performers, they will have more time and confidence to focus on complex bold strategies, perhaps new products and service offerings, new geographies, or entirely new markets. More empowered top performers and liberated leaders create an unstoppable combination. Excellence ensues.

The level and speed of play propels your organization to talent magnet status. The pool of talented individuals seems more like an ocean—opportunities to choose natural top performers seem to expand endlessly. Like the free agents who have signed with last year's champions to collaborate with other great players in an effort to win this year's championship, the best and the brightest leaders are drawn to the opportunity to work with bold people making bold bets. Top performers like to work with, and are attracted to, other top performers. That means that attracting top performers who then attract other top performers is critical to sustainable growth. Keep in mind that the depth of your organization's talent fleet determines the power with which it can grow.

Identify What You Need

Not all organizations understand exactly what they need in terms of talent. This is particularly true if an organization's leaders don't have a clear vision of growth. Without this vision, it's difficult to know what skills support a new, bold road map. Not knowing undermines confidence in both any investment in scouting talent and the talent's confidence in their ability to be successful. Managers don't look for the next talented individual because they don't currently have a need for her expertise or skills. But how are you to know what you need before you need it? By visualizing what you need to get started and finding people to talk to about what it will take. That means being curious and asking questions. Once your top and mid-level leaders are no longer enmeshed in the daily Run, they should be adopting a forward view. Recall from chapter 6 that that's what proactive improvements are about, and that's what building bold road maps involves. Having a forward view should enable them to begin to see further down the road and more broadly across the horizon. That's not to say that there won't be surprises. There will be many. A forward view, however, means that your Grow team should be able to anticipate at least a rudimentary shopping list of future needs.

Anticipating a more comprehensive list of future needs requires the ability to imagine both wild success and significant challenges. Imagine executing the strategy on a shoestring budget. There's nothing to engender resourcefulness like poverty. Imagine your Grow strategy is wildly successful. Anticipate how you will handle that success. What changes would that success require of your organization?

This is a modeling exercise, to be sure. Stress test success. You won't have data about your success when you're planning your success. You have to engage in positive contingency planning. Many fearful managers do downside contingency planning. Why not do more upside planning? As you develop contingency plans, remain flexible. Sometimes contingency plans can start to feel anchored in concrete, as they become increasingly detailed and begin to seem truly predictive. Remember that you're planning for possibilities, not eventualities; you need to stay flexible enough to respond, bend, and change in case the exact situation or need you anticipated doesn't come to pass but an unanticipated variation does.

Scout for Skills

Leaders should always be scouting for talent so that when the need for a certain skill arises, they can select bold people with that skill. In the Run-Improve-Grow system, **scouting** is being aware of, listening to, and watching out for talented top performers wherever they are. Those performers may—or *may not*—actively be seeking new opportunities. An essential part of talent scouting is looking for passive candidates as well as active ones. Your most compelling scouting resource should be your organization's new, bold road map. Share it with people; share it with customers; share it with suppliers. As talented people catch wind of your organization's innovative journey, they'll want to be a part of it. Think about it like this: When someone has told you that they're going to Rome, Paris, London, the Olympics, or the World Cup, one of your first responses has probably been, "Oh, I wish I were going with you!" Well, paint a vision of your organization's journey for talented top performers, and you'll be more likely to bring them along as part of your talent fleet.

As you share your story, ask your network questions specifically related to scouting:

- Who do you know who has picked the proverbial high-hanging fruit?
- We are seeking to innovate and expand in the following areas: __, __, and __. Who would know talented people who have the passion to explore with us?
- We're always looking for outstanding talent to challenge how we are doing business and going to market. Can you help me identify any top performers who would thrive on this challenge?

The wonderful thing about attracting talent and building a talent fleet is that talented individuals possess a variety of specific technical or work experience skills. Even one person's skills can make a difference to an organization's ability to flawlessly execute a new, bold road map. In the language of Run-Improve-Grow, there is a difference between skills and talents that leaders in the Run-Improve-Grow system need to keep in mind: **skills** are the knowledge and experience required to flawlessly execute a function; skills can be gained or taught. **Talents** are innate characteristics that maximize value in a variety of skills—a sense of urgency, intellectual curiosity, an analytical mind, and confidence are all talents from which any skilled function can benefit.

Leaders should look to more than learned skills. They should attract people with additional specific talents that can't be taught to most people. Here are a few talents that I have seen as critical to Run-Improve-Grow:

- Problem solving
- Desire to learn
- Fearlessness
- Self-confidence
- Empathy for others
- Stewardship of teamwork
- Initiative

Potential top performers with initiative add value to Grow teams. They understand current conditions in the marketplace and proactively engage existing and potential customers with solutions that trigger demand. Very often, top performers will stand out over the masses because they are confident in their problem-solving abilities and have empathy for others.

Remember our description of 10-80-10 as it related to raising the bar of excellence? In an early-stage company, top performers are generally utility players—they're naturally talented in many functions but not necessarily a master in specific functions. But after Run-Improve-Grow positions talented top performers in their most-value-added functions and the organization pivots into newer, bolder road maps, top-performer standards of excellence are redefined. Now there is room for multiple standards to reflect the variety of your top performers:

- Fearless and flawless frontline executor—reliable Run leader
- Proactive improvement system designer
- Curious innovator
- Rapid reactive improvement expert

Respect for the various talents and the development of deeper skills in each area are hallmarks of a professional organization and provide the foundation for a winning legacy.

Retaining the Best Talent

When organizations follow a Run-Improve-Grow journey and create a bold road map, they begin to attract exceptional talent. It's one thing to build a talent fleet, and it's quite another to keep it and expand it. Retaining driven talent is as important as attracting it. You retain those extremely talented people by accelerating good turnover and minimizing bad turnover.

There *are* times when turnover is an addition by subtraction. Near the end of the seven-year Run-Improve-Grow-journey period at one company, one top-performing leader was transferring into another division to lead organizational proactive improvements, so we faced a significant leadership gap that had to be filled. True to his nature, the top-performing leader even hired his replacement.

The replacement candidate said all of the right things in the interview process and possessed the right experience to indicate that he was a leader. The minute he stepped into the job, however, his performance and behavior showed that he was not a leader at all. Everything was about him. Big, BIG EGO. His previous experiences made him arrogant and closed to the ideas and suggestions of others. In a very short period of time, this single person was able to tear down the progress the company had made over seven years. I remember recommending a quick intervention to the president in the first week of Mr. Ego's employment. Unfortunately, it took eighteen months of organizational damage and employee defections before the egocentric leader was let go.

The lessons I learned from this experience are to:

- act quickly to reconcile hiring mistakes; and
- always nurture and protect a Run-Improve-Grow culture that has taken time to develop and become ingrained into an organization's DNA.

I also learned that cutting draggers is a desirable form of turnover—it's good turnover. When those people who have been pulling down the morale and performance of an organization finally leave, a wave of relief washes over the remaining members of the team. Or, at the very least, their departure barely causes a ripple within the organization, and in that case, you'll have reduced overhead. Cutting draggers is a case of addition by subtraction. It's better to cut draggers than to keep them on as deadweight pulling down the team or the organization as a whole.

Not all employee separations are cause for celebration, however. When top performers leave, it can be devastating to the organization. When a leader or top performer walks out on his remaining team members, that individual's actions scream, "We can't get it done here, so I'm going to find somewhere where my talents, skills, and effort contribute to victory." Such a sentiment is devastating to the personal beliefs of the remaining team members and requires leaders to spend time developing cohesion and trust in the new team and sparking integrated teamwork.

That kind of dysfunctional turnover relates directly to the organization's culture and prospects for growth. When an organization's top performers leave because of dysfunction in the organization, the impact of their departure is reflected negatively on remaining followers and draggers. Those who stay with the organization and witness talent leaving on a regular basis will feel cynical about the organization's future prospects and might even start to feel trapped.

The Run-Improve-Grow process helps leaders prevent dysfunctional turnover and the departure of top performers by eliminating the demotivating factors that may cause talented individuals to consider leaving.[1] Leaders hold the ability to unleash their employees' motivations—and inspire them to peak performance—or demotivate their employees and chase them off to other organizations.

The following table compares the factors that motivate individuals and teams to peak performance with those factors that compromise performance and perpetuate a cynical cycle.

PEAK PERFORMANCE	CYNICAL CYCLE
Creative autonomy	Micromanaging
Relationships of trust	Defensive interactions
Honesty	Hypocrisy
Ownership	Being owned
Hold yourself accountable	Hold others accountable
Mutual respect	Holier than thou
Robust communication	Out of the loop
Emotional discipline	Inconsistent behavior
Quality feedback	Closed-mindedness
Rewarding and removing obstacles for top performers	Spending time with and building systems around draggers
Zero trade-offs	Compromise
Relevance	Irrelevance
Proactive behavior	Reactive excuses
Timely information	Outdated data
Customer loyalty	Customer resentment
Talent fleet	Workers

Figure 9.1

When leaders work to eliminate demotivating factors, their employees are more prone to take ownership of their most-value-added performance functions.

How Do You Develop Bench Strength?

Bench strength is where talent attraction and talent retention meet. Even at the best, most progressive companies, people leave. They retire, have family issues, relocate to another part of the country, or set out to pursue other opportunities in completely different fields. Turnover is inevitable, so your sustainable growth organization needs to have a solid bench to fill talent gaps when required. So how can our organizations develop a deep and flexible bench? Developing bench strength requires a leadership mind-set that every employee is more capable than her title and prior experiences suggest. This must be one of the most important expectations of every leader.

Bench strength is having confidence in talented substitutes who can step into a certain function in someone else's absence. How deep your bench is will be determined, in part, by the volume and variety of bold bets you're making. It will also be determined by a mix of needs and available talent. Sometimes building a deep bench may defy traditional financial logic in the short term. That's why there's an art to building a bench that relies on leadership skills and vision. Companies spend millions on hard assets, such as inventory, equipment, buildings, and so on, long before they really need them to succeed. Until the work comes in, those investments are passive and not yielding results. What if organizations planned the same way with regard to their people? What if companies anticipated their need for skills and talents— and invested accordingly in people in advance? Those investments wouldn't be passive, however, because people can learn and contribute *before* they're needed.

Bench strength is more than just hiring or attracting talent; it's also about proactively positioning people within the organization to develop future skills. To build a strong bench from the talent you have, you need to eliminate limitations and encourage employees to take on more—and more meaningful— responsibilities. You want to give them the opportunity to work their muscles, so to speak. Otherwise, their skills and talents remain weak.

Eliminate Limitations

One way to develop bench strength is to eliminate employee limitations. One year, while I was working at Johnson & Johnson, Alan Oak, a mechanical engineering student at the University of Cincinnati, was having lunch with other students working at the company as part of a co-op program through the university. Most of these co-op student workers were being asked to do paperwork and collect data by the engineers they were assigned to work with. That didn't seem to be what a co-op program was supposed to deliver to the students. When I worked as a UPS engineering co-op, I was stretched beyond what I thought possible. Awesome!

I sensed some uninspired co-op students complaining about their menial assignments. I asked, "Who'd like to work on some tough problems?" Alan stepped up right away. We didn't even bother to ask who he was assigned to or what work would be derailed by having him on my project. I trusted Alan would make sure he met his other commitments. Alan was challenged to solve some of the hardest problems that many experienced engineers hadn't been able to conquer for years. He knew that, too. Why not allow him to gain experience and confidence by achieving something others couldn't? This taught him how to manage a complex project, train others on new processes, develop new systems, and create new testing methods for our systems and processes.

Alan was never treated like a co-op student or an intern; rather, he was treated like a smart and talented peer who had the capacity to do much more than even he believed he could do. The key was that he didn't know what he *couldn't* do, so he was allowed to try-storm anything and then come to me when he was stumped. He was fearless and yet knew he was supported. He was trusted and was trusting. That experience was valuable for Alan, for the organization, and for me. Alan continues to eliminate barriers for his teams as a very successful leader who says that experience shaped him.

From a bench-strength perspective, leaders have to make sure they don't create employee limitations based on titles or expectations. Leaders can't be afraid if their team surpasses them. To realize the most out of every employee's talent, leaders must challenge employees to go beyond what they believe they can do, and then use the results as a measuring stick for an individual's potential and propensity to learn going forward.

Push Employees to Sink or Swim

Top performers aren't the only team members who should be expected to jump in a bit over their heads. You also need to give others the opportunity to push their limits because, realistically, no strong bench is comprised entirely of top performers. For example, leaders should encourage a reliable executor who likes numbers to not only create and file a report, but to also provide an analysis of the report and implement it. At first, leaders and/ or top performers need to be present to coach individuals (as they need a vision of what success looks like), but the point is that even those individuals who don't possess the innate talents of a top performer can still be led to higher levels of performance in their daily execution. Leaders should always encourage employees to move outside of a traditional function's box. Say, "Be fearless and come to me with several solutions!"

Our behaviors with our team matter! Your team has members who will be the future leaders of many organizations. As their leader now, you need to provide them with phenomenal coaching—not just problem-solving, analytical, or financial management skills. Help them gain the self-confidence to try something new that is not a part of their previous experiences. Be patient in your teaching at the same time you challenge people beyond what they think is possible. Above all, do it in a way that is positive and engaging. The key is to believe each person has unlimited potential and that it's your role and responsibility to tap into it and draw out the best from each of them.

When developing bench strength, leaders should push their employees into the deep end but still be the lifeguard who will make sure they don't drown. When the majority of employees display the capability to perform a function on their own, the leader can focus his attention on something or someone else.

What's just as important as giving everyone more incremental responsibilities in existing functions is seeing how well they take it. Leaders want to create an environment not necessarily where the masses are *given* incremental responsibilities but where they begin to *take* incremental responsibilities on their own.

Play to Strengths

Developing bench strength requires developing individual players' strengths. Rather than focusing on improving weaknesses, focus on maximizing strengths and minimizing the effects of the weaknesses. That is at the heart of the most-value-added principle. At the same time, you need to be careful not to create a full bench of players who have the same strength. You want variety. In fact, strength comes from that variety.

No winning team has all quarterbacks or all pitchers or all goalies. You can't build a company by putting everyone on the front line or at the front door. To elevate your organization's performance from little league to professional, you need to develop the unique skills of each person to the highest level rather than develop general skills across the board. All professional athletes have a basic level of conditioning and strength, but beyond that they have honed skills in areas that relate to their particular position and their role on the field or court. Likewise, as organizations develop and increase their level of play, so to speak, the roles in the company change and evolve. So as businesses Grow from G_1 to G_2 to G_3, those roles must adjust dramatically—as should the depth of skills and talents each person needs to succeed at the highest level.

Organizations that encourage this evolution and development become talent magnets for the best people to fill those evolving roles. Top performers want to maintain their level of excellence, so they seek to be a part of the best organizations—the ones that demonstrate the willingness to invest in breakthrough learning and development. Think about it. Leaders in areas like mobile application programming, alternative fuel research, advanced welding engineering, microbiology, and cancer research aren't interested in becoming the best executor of your organization's daily Run. They are seeking advanced skills and knowledge so they can become the best in their field. If you have those people in your organization and insist they develop general business skills most needed by those in the Run, you're actively preventing those talented people from developing their most-value-added skills and abilities. Not only are you preventing them from maximizing their MVA and from mastery, you're preventing the entire organization from innovating. How demotivating! Unfortunately, too many organizations do this every day.

Numerous tools and techniques exist to help you to identify and maximize your team's strengths, both on an individual and collective level. For information about some of these tools, visit the Resources tab of rayattiyah.com.

Why a Deep Bench Matters to Run-Improve-Grow

What's critical to understand about bench strength is that the roles needed and expectations for them change over time. As organizations fulfill bold promises and place bolder and bolder bets, the standards of what is considered exceptional escalate. The organization's talent has to raise its standards in unison. At the risk of overplaying the sports analogy: you've got to have a solid playbook and be able to score from the bench.

Widespread growth and success don't come from having a couple of star players as part of an otherwise average team. You need to have a strong team across the board to really win those bold bets and capitalize on incredible opportunities. As you cultivate more growth opportunities, you are going to want to have available a wide variety of strengths. Variety in talent, strengths, and perspective is what will invest your growth with a richness that a single-minded or weak bench cannot produce.

Run-Improve-Grow started with people and their behaviors. And now, at this stage of the process, when we're starting over for R_2, we're again shining the light on the need for talented, strong, innovative, and creative people whose behaviors and attitudes reflect the new RIG culture. Without those people to engage— and without engaging those people—Run-Improve-Grow cannot be optimized. Because Run-Improve-Grow is iterative, you can't effectively launch into R_2 with only the same talents and skills required to lock in your R_1. (You may have the same people, but the talents and skills need to be more advanced.) R_2 needs to be designed with the vision of G_2. By definition, growth leads to new states of being and working. The needs of a growing organization are not the same as those of a young organization or, indeed, of a declining or stagnant one.

Building a strong bench matters because it minimizes the risk of mediocrity. Strong players are less apt to tolerate unacceptable performance from their teammates. They do more than their best and they expect the same of the team. The organization benefits by having a systemic ally against the cynical cycle and detrimental personal beliefs. A talent fleet that has bench strength is a purposeful plan for the human resources that power your organization. It's also their energy source.

Talent is the linchpin for transformational growth. No organization can Grow beyond where it is without involving talented people who can help it achieve ever-higher levels of excellence. Your job as a leader is to be constantly scouting talent both inside and outside the organization. That way, when you're ready to simplify and solidify R_2, you have the right people in the right place on your team.

Think of your best coaches and teachers. Did they let you get away with mediocrity? No. They challenged you to do things you'd never done before and supported you along the way. And that's why you consider them to be great coaches or teachers.

Now it's your turn to go out and be a great coach, teacher,

mentor, and leader to everyone in your organization. Harness the power of your people so they truly *want* to be there, working among other talented top performers. Inspire your people to tell others how great it is to work at your organization. Give your people the simplest road to individual and organizational peak performance, but don't settle for what's easy. Be fearless but not reckless. Give those around you a unified vision and purpose for organizational peak performance. Then, find ways to help them maximize their strengths to spark your organization's confidence. The result will be that the best and brightest will flock to your door, your website, and your social media pages in hopes of finding their way into your organization to help them achieve their bold growth. And that's the foundation you need for a lifetime of sustainable growth as a Run-Improve-Grow organization.

TAKEAWAYS

- If people are our most valuable assets and talent drives organizational peak performance, top-performing organizations need to be talent magnets.
- To assemble a talent fleet, you've got to up your game. When your organization becomes a top-performing organization, talented individuals will want to join you.
- As your company changes and Grows, its leaders must intentionally think about the skills and talents it needs to continue to Improve and innovate and be on the lookout for people with those skills and talents.
- For organizations to truly Grow, they need to attract extremely talented people—and keep them on board and growing themselves.
- Part of retaining talented people involves accelerating good turnover and minimizing bad turnover.

(continued)

- Top performers always want to win, so they join the organizations that provide an opportunity for success.
- Developing bench strength is critical as your organization seeks to take advantage of new growth opportunities outside the drip line.
- Attracting top performers who then attract other top performers is critical to sustainable growth, because the depth of an organization's talent fleet determines the power with which it can innovate.
- Developing bench strength requires a leadership mind-set that every employee is more capable than her title or prior experiences suggest. Bench strength is having confidence in talented substitutions to step into a certain function in someone else's absence.
- Bench strength is more than just hiring or attracting talent; it's also about proactively positioning people within the organization to develop future skills.
- Becoming a talent magnet is what enables growth-driven organizations to realize perpetual Run-Improve-Grow.

TO: <ALL EMPLOYEE E-MAIL LIST>

FROM: Liberated.Leader@RIG_company.com

Dear Team,

Wow, I don't know what to say. Yesterday's meeting with a customer really brought to light all that you've accomplished in the past year. The past twelve months have been amazing! A year ago I was thinking about all the problems we had, all the improvements that needed to be made, and whether we could do it. I received an e-mail this morning from our customer telling me how much better it is doing business with us than any other supplier. It was a comment on how impressed they are with our team, our energy, and our excitement. The one word she used over and over again to describe what she saw in our team was "pride."

The level of energy we have now is amazing. Several of you asked me last week if we were going to continue allowing everyone to keep making changes and improvements. The short answer is "Yes." As we continue to move forward and upward, we must be very vigilant and not be satisfied to stop at our recent success. The new project that came in last week shows that we have to keep on bringing in new talent and new work to Grow.

Right now I can't tell you how proud I am of us as a team, how well we collaborate, and how we challenge each other in a very respectful way. Our systems now support us, our technology supports our work, and everyone has the tools needed to succeed. Your ownership of the Run and the way you hold yourselves accountable have been the drivers of this new greatness. You've given us the courage to draft bold and dramatic growth plans. By being fearless, you have inspired our managers to undertake even bolder proactive improvements and not get sucked back into the Run. We have to be vigilant about keeping work simple and keeping bureaucracy at bay.

We have two choices: (1) We can be happy we're on top, or (2) we can make a game of topping ourselves. We choose number two. Our best and brightest demand that we keep challenging ourselves. We must not lose sight of the fact that many people have greater potential and desire to learn. We must continue to cultivate talent and excellence at all levels.

We have come a long way in twelve months. People are finding more success in the roles that they're in now. Together, we've solved a lot of problems and overcome the obstacles that prevented our company from truly growing. We've set a new, innovative, and creative path for ourselves by evolving. We will not stop evolving. We will not stop growing. And our recent success shows that we don't have to compromise between growth, profitability, customer satisfaction, and our enjoyment.

I am really encouraged by the new culture of our company, one that emphasizes constant improvement and innovation. I congratulate you for your part in creating it, and I look forward to working with you to keep it vibrant and dynamic. How fun it is to come to work again!

Endnotes

Chapter 1

1. Note that does not assume that the remaining 15 percent are mid-tier or top managers. There are other positions (staff, support, etc.) that are included in that figure as well.

Chapter 2

1. If you aren't sure of the strengths of your individual team members or you need help facilitating the process, there are numerous assessment tools available to help you. For a list of options, see rayattiyah.com.

Chapter 3

1. The coaching relationship between the trainer and the frontline leader is critical in the leader's development. The bond needs to be built on mutual trust and respect because the frontline leader will ultimately be stepping out in front of everyone around them into a very vulnerable spotlight.

2. This method comes from executive coach Elaine Seuss, who also organized the talent-development resources on rayattiyah.com.

Chapter 4

1. Note that I'm not using the word *unmotivated*, which implies that there is no current motivation but doesn't give any insight into whether the person had previously been motivated. *Unmotivated* simply indicates a lack of motivation. I'm purposefully using the word *demotivated*, which indicates a decrease in motivation; that is to say, someone who is demotivated was once motivated.

2. Thanks to Jason Lockwood for explaining the relationship between organizational energy and sparks in this practical way. He suggested that every physical body wants to rest at its lowest energy state.

3. This might seem like the sawtooth effect from chapter 1, but that refers to an organization's actual output—employee performance, revenue, operational efficiency. The energy continuum is about how much energy it takes to get to new levels.

Chapter 6

1. Like draggers, laggards may never adopt new ideas. It's as if they think we should all still be using carbon copies because they worked just fine. You can almost hear them saying, "Why do *I* need to learn to *type?*"

Chapter 7

1. Quote from the "Say Yes" video segment from *Small Business School*, a PBS show about small and medium businesses. For more about Mike Neary and the bold moves of Oregon Log Home Company, check out http://smallbusinessschool.org.

Chapter 8

1. A skunkworks involves organizing a group of people to implement a high-priority project whose goal is radical innovation. The team is independent and has the freedom to really go bold.

2. Grow teams in Run-Improve-Grow are also not necessarily merger and acquisition teams. Organizations can Grow by acquiring other businesses, but the focus of Run-Improve-Grow is to develop the Grow organically from inside the organization first. Depending on the opportunities your organization wants to pursue, you might need to acquire companies with particular competencies. Any such activity, however, should be a means to an end, not the end itself.

3. Ron Stibich's team originated the term *innovation spark*, and it's a perfect reflection of what happens in Run-Improve-Grow.

Chapter 9

1. I like to say that people leave organizations, but they quit bosses. If you're losing highly talented people, examine the reporting structures in your company to see if any patterns emerge.

Acknowledgments

Over 500,000 man-hours were invested in training, research, trials, learning, and honing of the practical system that is in this book. Beyond our team's efforts, so many others helped make this book a reality. It would be difficult for me to express my gratitude to all of them here.

I first want to thank my colleagues for providing leadership and acting fearlessly to create an outstanding team, product, and future: Tara Amis, Dan D'Agostino, John D'Agostino, John Harvey, Kevin Linehan, Dave Mills, Ed Robinson, Dave Satcher, and Tricia Rigsby. Likewise, the dedication of the Definity Partners' team, alumni, and spouses have produced and supported many fearless frontline leaders and business successes. Thanks to Brian Besl, Rich Cary, Dave Bishop, Keith Daniel, Eric Collet, Shawn Flynn, Matt Higgins, Brian Neumann, Bob Owen, Rick Richkowski, Bill Rouse, Adam Snyder, and Nick Williams. Kyle Brandon, Joe Chandler, Bob Clague, Jerry Combs, Brian Cunningham, Bonnie DiGiacomo, Todd Eppert, Dave Fulton, Lori Harding, Tim Holman, Paul Kopelson, Jennifer Kist, Jay Kuhn, Scott Luton, Christina Mann, Mike McBride, Emma Mills, Dale Mitchell, Jeff Muskopf, Michelle Renn, Allison Rogers, and Tom Shaw.

Thanks to Gary Allen, Jay Tepe, and Don Gould for believing in your front line in 1996 and lighting the spark. The personal guidance of Ron Stibich, Doug Sutton, Mike Bull, Jason Lockwood, Greg Simko, Fabian Schmahl, Matt Chestnut, and Cheri Stevenot inspired me to be courageous and to never settle. Thank you.

I also want to thank those who invested their personal time

reading previous manuscripts and providing honest feedback and valuable insight. Rick Alley, Page Busken, Karen Bankston, Jim Barney, Sue Bingham, Ruth Ann Church, Heidi Coble, Mike Collinsworth, Kevin Dickey, Dave Flynn, Margaret Grayson, Doug Herald, Kim Hill, Carter Johnson, George Leasure, Sally Missimi, Mike Nemeth, Susan Osborne, Chris Painter, Debbie Pearce, Mindy Taylor, Dale Vernon, John Yengo —your contributions helped shape this book and more. A special thanks to Tim Berridge, Kevin Mackey, and Steve Watkins who trystormed with me on three previous drafts of the book. Were it not for their diligence and commitment, I'd still be writing the rough manuscript.

During those 500,000 man-hours, many people provided positive leadership behaviors and valuable support of our developing organization. Thank you. The experiences we shared helped forge the system that is Run-Improve-Grow. I look forward to innovating the future together: Doug Alexander, Skip Allan, Gary Armstrong, Tom Begg, Joe Bornhorst, Frank Carella, David Caudill, Jerry Cole, Kevyn Coy, Mike Crane Tanny Crane, Dan Cunningham, Dave Damon, Jeff Dawley, Art Dierks, Joe Eramo, Larry Estes, Ron Estes, Mark Farmer, Fidelity's AQP Gold Medal teams, Jon Geisler, John Gimpel, Jon Gimpel, Jeff Gleich, Tom Glomski, Louis Goldner , Tom Gramlich, David Hall, Dave Harry, Mark Hartings, Bill Herkamp, Ron Heygesi, Steve Hinds, Dan Hogan, Stu Kemper, David Knowles, Mark Leasure, Chip Lennon, Jim Lilly, Steve Lotz, Bill O'Gara, Alan Page, Lynette Peters, Mike Ponder, Troy Post, Walt Rice, Mark Rippe, Durk Rorie, Doug Smith, Mike Smith, Ginger Timberlake, Wendy Vonderhaar, Lou Vilardo, J. Wright, Dan Yinger, and Jim Ziminski.

In 2009, when markets and pundits saw no hope for manufacturing in America, Kevin Sharp, Amy Gogul, Sean Faller, Ben Doan, Bill Carroll and the Upside Innovations team instead made a bold bet on America's manufacturing sector. When they started a manufacturing company, I was (and still am) honored that they chose Run-Improve-Grow as their start-up system.

I also want to acknowledge Bonnie Younker, Sue Gibson, Rose Fletcher, the third-shift team members, Dick Tohline, Dennis Hutchinson, Bob Salerno, Bob Brede, John McFadden, Wayne Morrison, Crystal Morrison, Wendy Scaggs, Veronica Manuel, Alan Oak, and David MacKenzie for creating a fearless, challenging, and energizing environment at Johnson & Johnson. That environment provided the foundation that supported the development of Run-Improve-Grow. Many thanks to Ron Carson, Gary Powers, Chuck Harrell, Greg Swartz, and so many others for showing me the power and potential of a fearless front line.

This book wouldn't be here today without Jamie Bryant. Jamie is my "new talent" to help me with my Grow. Thank you, Jamie and your talented team at B-books, for your passion, patience, and great questions that guided the creation of this book and so much more. I also want to thank our publisher, Bibliomotion, whose team poured what they've learned though hundreds of successes into this book. Thanks also to Mo Elghamri, for his fearless product development, and to Annie Radel, who is quite simply, fearless. Without Annie's diligence, persistence, and organizational skills, so many practical aspects of getting a book to market would still be waiting to be done. Thank you, Annie.

A very special acknowledgment to the family of the late Josh Weve. In 2007, Josh reminded me that our work is one small part of our lives. Josh was motivated to improve his daily work so that he could spend quality time with his kids and be a great dad. To me, nothing is more inspiring.

Read and hear more about these and other leaders @ rayattiyah .com/thankyou

Index

A
accountability, 73
adoption process, 117–118
Allen, David, 28–29
Allen, Gary, 152–153, 164
Amazon, 110–111, 112–113
ambiguity, 113–114
answers, not having all, 16–17
apathy, 69–70
assumptions, 157
AT&T, 139
attitudes, 21–22, 93
authoritarian managers, 17–18
authority, 83

B
behavior modeling, 45
    daily huddles and, 47, 48, 50–51
    management systems and, 84–85
    momentum transfer through, 63,
        65–66
    of quick action, 65–66
    transitioning leadership through,
        52–54
beliefs, negative personal, 10–12,
    15–16
bench strength, 187–190
bets, bold, 155–175
    capitalizing on the biggest,
        162–166

fail fast, go big, 162–163
Grow teams and, 169–171
grow teams and, 166–171
identifying best, 156, 160–162
importance of, 171–174
large vs. small opportunities and,
    156, 159–160
learning from successes and,
    156–158
managing outside the drip line,
    164–166
organizational health/purpose and,
    172–174
past successes/failures and,
    156–159
sure bets, 156–162
BlackBerry, 135
bold bets. *See* bets, bold
bold promises. *See* promises, bold
brainstorming, 124
breakdown points, identifying, 28
burnout, 20–21
business development, 83

C
calmness, 31
cellular devices, 138–139, 172
change
    deadly behaviors for, 69–71
    obstacles to, 66–68

change (*continued*)
  readiness for, 121–122
  resistance to, 27–28, 66–67
  thought leaders and, 119–121
change models, 67–68
clique behavior, 70
clutter. *See* complexity
coaching, 188–189
collaboration. *See also* teams
  Grow teams and, 166–171
  mind-set for, 46
  momentum and, 77
  quick wins and, 46
  standards and, 74–75
  trust and, 11, 35
  "Yes we can," 142–145
comfort zones, 16, 86, 165–166
commoditization, 126, 147
communication
  collaboration and, 77
  cross-functional, 74–76
  daily huddles and, 47, 48–49, 50–51
  from lack of confidence/trust, 83–84
  layered systems of, 93–94
  leadership behavior and, 53
  management systems and, 83, 87, 93–94
  managing outside the drip line and, 165–166
  relationship building and, 11–12
  of standards, 26
  teamwork and, 74–76
compassion, 30
compensation plans. *See* reward systems
competition, 97–98
  bold promises and, 151
  quality and reliability and, 139
  rate of improvement and, 133–135
competitive advantages, 148
competitive landscape, 122–123, 161
complexity, 107–108

in communication, 93–94
confidence and, 135
institutionalization of unnecessary, 14
lack of confidence and, 83–84
resistance to eliminating, 27–28
sawtooth effect and, 7
simplifying processes and, 27–29
unnecessary, 3, 14, 28–29
unreliable systems/processes and, 13–15
compliance, 40–41, 200
compromises, 135–137, 168–169
confidence, 26, 38
  attracting employees and, 181
  bench strength and, 187–191
  bold promises and, 131–154, 152–153
  compromise and, 135–137
  conveying in questions, 88
  customer, 134–135
  customer relationships and, 140–145
  daily huddles and, 51–52
  lack of in Run-centric cultures, 10–11, 83–84
  leadership and, 30–31
  opportunity costs and, 140
  poor performers and, 34
  in processes and systems, 13–15
  quick wins and, 45
Consumer Reports, 138
continuous improvement, 82, 109. *See also* proactive improvements
courage, 28
credibility, 146–147
crisis situations, 65
cross-functional integration, 76–79
Crossing the Chasm (Moore), 118
culture
  bold bets and, 171, 172–174, 173–174

cynical, 21–22
fearless, 23–36
hiring and, 184
management systems and, 86–87
Run-centric, 9–10
curiosity, 151
customers
bold bets and, 173
bold promises and, 133–135
complaints of, bold promises and, 133
compromise and, 135–137
confidence of, 134–135
entropy in, 145–147
focusing on, 23–36
focus on satisfaction of, 46
Grow teams and, 166–171
proactive improvements and, 110–112, 116
quality and, 137–140
reliability and, 138–139
cynical cycle, 21–22, 35, 66, 186
cynicism, 69–70

D
daily huddles, 38, 47–52
huddle boards and, 49–50
leading, 50–52
reviewing successes and failures in, 156–159
decision-making systems, 70–71
delegating, 6–7, 177
dependence, 18, 21
design failures, 158–159
differentiation, 139, 147
diffusion process, 117–118
direction, 83
disruptive market approaches, 111
distrust, 10, 12. See also trust
drip line, managing outside, 164–166
due diligence, 160–161, 162

E
early adopters, 117–118
empathy, 30, 183
employees
attitudes of shaped by managers, 21
attracting the best, 153, 176, 178–184
bench strength with, 187–191
bold bets and, 161–162, 173
cynical, 69–70
in cynical cycle, 21–22
daily huddles and, 51–52
delegating responsibility to, 6–7
developing, 33–34, 35
draggers, 43
effects of high-performing, 39–41
future need for, 181
in Grow teams, 166–171
higher-performing, focus on, 33–34, 38–44
hiring decisions and, 102–103
identifying needed, 180–181
importance of in Run-Improve-Grow, 190–192
limitations on, eliminating, 187–188
losing talented, 126, 184–185
maintaining talent fleet of, 178
negative beliefs of managers about, 10–12
perceptions of marathon managers, 17–20
performance levels of, 39
playing to strengths of, 190–191
poorly performing, 33–34
pushing to sink or swim, 189–190
quick wins for, 38, 44–47
raising the bar for, 38–44
recognizing high-performing, 43
retaining, 177, 184–186
Run-centric cultures and, 10–15
scouting, 161–162, 176–202

employees (*continued*)
  skill deficiencies in, 54
  skills of, scouting for, 182–184
  strengths of, identifying, 25–26
  training, 44, 52–56
  transitioning leadership to
    top-performing, 52–56
  turnover in, 184–185
empowerment, 109
  attracting employees and,
    178–179
  daily huddles and, 38, 47–52
  of front line, 37–58
  modeling and, 54–55
  quick wins and, 44–47
  raising the bar and, 41–42
energy, organizational, 72–73. *See also*
    momentum
engagement, 11–12, 72, 73
  purpose and, 173–174
entrepreneurs, 167
entropy, 61, 145–147
Evercoat, 169–170
excellence
  daily huddles and, 47, 49, 50–51
  raising the bar and, 38–44, 49
execution
  bold promises and, 131–154
  failures in, 158–159
expectations, 145–147
experimentation, 56

F
failure, causes of, 158–159
fast followers, 126
fear,
  bold promises and, 133
  as motivator, 95
  proactive improvements and, 115
fearless cultures
  developing, 23–36

elements of, 29–31
eliminating marathon managers
  and, 23–29
impediments to, 32–34
importance of, 34–35
most-value-added functions and,
  24–26
proactive improvements and,
  112–114
raising the bar in, 38–44
in the Run, developing, 38–52
simplifying the Run in, 26–29
takeaways on, 36
fearlessness, 183
FedEx, 135–136, 151
feedback, 116
financial results, 172
  Run-Improve-Grow and, 9–10
  talent fleet and, 178
flexibility, 85–86
focus
  competitive landscape and,
    122–123, 125
  customer-based, 23–36, 134–135
  on high performers, 33–34
  internal, 133–135
  in questions, 88–91
  on though leaders, 119–121
follow-through, 118–119
Fort Wilderness Lodge, 131–132
forward thinking, 123–125
front line
  authoritarian managers and,
    17–18
  daily huddles and, 38, 47–52
  empowering, 37–58
  integrated teamwork in, 75–76
  quick-wins for, 38, 44–47
  sawtooth effect and, 4–7
  transitioning Run leadership to,
    37–38
functional silos, 67–68

G
gatekeepers, 17–18
General Electric, 152–153
Getting Things Done: The Art of Stress-Free Productivity (Allen), 28–29
goals, 103
    Grow teams and, 170–171
    for proactive improvements, 113
Grow, 129–193. *See also* Run-Improve-Grow
    bold promises and, 131–154
    employee talent and, 177–194
    proactive improvements and, 108
    teams, 166–171, 177–194
    time allocation for, 5–10
growth
    bold promises and, 147–150
    transformational, 126
    unpredictable, 67

H
hedging, 146–147
hierarchy of needs, 96–97, 100
highest and best use. *See* most-value-added (MVA) functions
Hoarders (TV show), 27–28
huddle boards, 49–50, 54
huddles, daily. *See* daily huddles
humility, 31
hypervigilance, 19–20

I
ignorance, 133
Improve, 15, 59–128. *See also* Run-Improve-Grow
    goal of, 109
    management system upgrades and, 81–106
    manager role in, 15
    momentum in, 61–80
    proactive improvements in, 107–128
    time allocation for, 5–10
improvement projects, 177
information gathering, 160–161, 162
infrastructure, proactive improvements and, 109–112, 125
initiative, in employees, 182
initiatives
    choosing, 46–47
innovation and innovators, 117–118, 119–121, 131–132
    bold promises and, 132–137, 146–147
    customers in, 144–145
    employee talent fleet and, 177
    growth driven by, 140
    managing outside the drip line and, 165–166
    relevance and, 150–153
    sustainability and, 132
integrated teamwork, 75–76, 84–85
integration, cross-functional, 76–79
irrelevance, 147

J
Johnson & Johnson, 187
Jung, Carl, 200

K
Kindle, 111, 112–113

L
laggards, 126
layoffs, 177
leadership
    communication and, 93–94
    creating new style for, 87–103
    culture of, 73–74

leadership (*continued*)
  in daily huddles, 38, 47–52
  definition of, 29–30
  empowering front line, 37–58
  expectations of, 107–108
  fearless culture and, 32–34
  importance of transitioning, 56–57
  momentum and, 65–66, 73–74
  motivation and, 100–102
  poor performers and, 33–34
  priorities and, 87–93
  raising the bar through, 38–44
  role of in organizations, 31
  skills and, 32–33
  talent assets and, 161–162
  traits in, 30–31
  transitioning to top performers,
    37–38, 52–56
  wrong people in, 32–33
logistics, 83
lonely wedge, 19–20

M

management models, 46
management systems, 81–106
  communication and, 87, 93–94
  creating new leadership styles for,
    87–103
  definition of, 83
  impact of faulty, 82–85
  importance of upgrading,
    103–105
  priorities and, 87–93
  reward systems and, 87, 94–103
managers
  authoritarian, 17–18
  in cynical cycle, 21–22
  daily huddles and, 38, 47–52
  eliminating marathon, 23–29
  employee perceptions of marathon,
    17–20

focus on performance for, 33–34,
    42–43
  impact of marathon, 20–22
  leaders and, 30–31
  management systems and, 81–106
  managing outside the drip line,
    164–166
  micro-, 10–15
  most-value-added functions of,
    6–7, 24–26
  negative personal beliefs of, 10–12,
    15–16
  resources wasted by, 56–57
  role of in organizations, 31
  in Run-centric cultures, 10–15
  sawtooth effect and, 4–7
  stretched beyond capacity, 19–20
  superfluous systems/processes and,
    13–15
market knowledge, 122–123, 161
market leadership, 126
Maslow, Abraham, 96–97, 100
matrix, opportunity analysis, 159–160
mediocrity, 40–41, 69–70, 126,
    191–192
meetings, extra, 83, 84
mentoring, 55–56, 188–189
metrics
  flawed, 69–71
  proactive improvements and,
    116–117
micromanagment, 10–15, 18
milestones, 170–171
mind-set, 46, 162, 163–164
mobile communication, 138–139
modeling. *See* behavior modeling
momentum, 61–80
  deadly behaviors for, 69–71
  importance of transferring, 76–79
  management systems and, 84
  operations and, 63–64
  from quick wins, 61, 63–64, 66–68

quick wins and, 66–68
roadblocks to, 64–71
transferring between operational
    areas, 71–76
Moore, Geoffrey, 118
most-value-added (MVA) functions,
    6–7, 24–26
  fearless cultures and, 32
  management systems and, 85–87
  prioritizing, 92–93
motivation, 39
  external vs. internal, 95
  higher-level, 98–103
  momentum and, 66–67
  money as, 95–98
  performance vs. cynicism and, 185
  questions for discovering, 101–102
  quick wins and, 66–67
  transferring momentum and, 61–80
MVA. *See* most-value-added (MVA)
    functions
Myers-Briggs, 200

N
Neary, Mike, 131–132, 142, 145
needs, hierarchy of, 96–97, 100
negative complexity, 3, 13–14. *See also*
    complexity
negativity, 69–70
nonjudgment, 31
norms, 51–52

O
Oak, Alan, 187
obstacles, quick wins and, 48
operations
  bold promises and, 148
  momentum in, 63–64
  optimization of, 64
  time spent managing, 4–10

opportunities, 155–175
  capitalizing on the biggest,
      162–166
  large vs. small, 156, 159–160
  triage for, 156, 160–162
opportunity costs, 34, 140
optimization, operational, 64, 67–68
Oregon Log Home Company,
    131–132, 142, 145
organizational energy, 72–73
organizational health, 172–174
organizational structure, 61–63,
    70–71, 83
overhead costs, 127
ownership, 72, 73

P
passion, as motivator, 98–103
peer pressure, 95, 97–98
performance
  attracting employees and,
      178–180
  control vs., 31
  effects of top employees on, 39–41,
      184–185
  focus on high, 33–34
  huddle boards and, 49–50
  leaders in inspiring, 30–31
  peak, 25–26
  quick wins and, 38, 44–47
  raising the bar for, 38–44
  remediation of poor, 33–34
  simplification and, 28–29
  standards and, 26, 75
  10-80-10 focus for, 119–121
perspective, changing, 46, 162,
    163–164
pipelines, 161
playing not to lose, 16, 17
predictability, 148, 165
priorities, 83, 87–93

proactive improvements, 107–128
    adoption of, 117–119
    competitive landscape and, 122–123
    consequences of ignoring, 126–127
    definition of, 108
    follow-through with, 118–119
    forward thinking and, 123–125
    implementing, 119–125
    importance of, 125–127
    measuring, 116–117
    reactive improvements vs., 109–114
    resistance to, 115–116
    risk levels and, 112–114
    what they simplify, 109–112
    what to expect in, 114–115
problem-solving
    as critical skill, 182
    daily huddles and, 48
    employee investment in, 35
    forward thinking and, 123–125
processes
    change models and, 67–68
    developing, 35
    identifying unnecessary, 28–29
    readiness for change in, 121–122
    simplifying, 26–29
    superfluous, as safety nets, 13
    unreliable, in Run-centric cultures,
        12–15
productivity, desire for, 10
project plans, 157
promises, bold, 131–154
    compromise vs., 135–137
    credibility and, 146–147
    customer relationships and, 140–145
    fear and, 133
    growth driven by, 147–150
    importance of, 145–153
    internal focus and, 133–135
    relevance and, 150–153
    reliability and quality and, 137–145
purpose, 98–103, 172–174

Q
quality, 137–140
    customer relationships and, 140–145
    standards of, 139–140
questions
    for finding quick wins, 48
    in function identification, 91–92
    high performers and, 43
    management priorities and, 87–93
    on motivation, 101–102
    to reinforce leadership behavior, 53
    solution-oriented, 88
    "What if…", 123, 124–125
quick wins, 38, 44–47
    choosing, 46–47
    momentum from, 61, 63–64,
        66–68, 71–76
    in operations, 63–64
    performance-based, 47
    real improvement from, 64–65
    top performers and, 74
    treating like projects, 66–68
    uncovering opportunities for, 48

R
rapport, 30
reactive improvements, 26, 27,
        107–108
    breakdown points and, 28
    definition of, 108
    proactive improvements vs.,
        109–114
relationships
    customer, 140–145
    high-performing employees and,
        42–43
    identifying employee strengths
        through, 25–26
    motivation and, 101–102
    transitioning leadership and, 53
    trust and, 11–12, 35

relevance, 150–153, 152–153
  bold bets and, 171–172
reliability, 137–140, 165
  customer relationships and,
    140–145
  standards of, 139–140
remediation, 33–34
resistance, 27–28, 69–71
  internal, 115–116
  to proactive improvement, 115–116
resource management, 172
respect, 31, 43
responsibility
  delegating, 6–7
  transitioning to employees, 37–38
reward systems, 39, 83, 87, 94–103
  fairness of, 101
  misaligned, 69–71
  money as motivator and, 95–98
risk
  bold bets and, 172
  calculated, taking, 156–162
  proactive improvements and,
    112–114
road maps, 172–174
Run, 3–58
  definition of, 14
  detaching from, 92–93
  empowering the front line for,
    37–58
  fearless culture for, 23–36, 38–52
  marathon managers and, 3–22
  most-value-added functions and,
    24–26
  operations in, 63–64
  questions focused on, 88–89
  simplifying, 26–29
  superfluous systems/processes and,
    13–15
  time allocation for, 5–10
  transitioning leadership for, 37–38
  what pulls managers into, 15–17

Run-centric cultures, 22
  disadvantages of, 9–10
  how they develop, 10–15
  negative personal beliefs in, 10–12
  unreliable systems and processes
    in, 12–15
Run-Improve-Grow, 5–7
  customer confidence and, 134–135
  dream stage of, 149–150
  drivers behind use of, 107–108
  iterations of, 104–105
  management systems and, 103–105
  resistance to, 27–28
  sustainability of, 7
  systemic approach in, 67–68
  time allocation in, 7–10

S
sales, confidence in, 142–145
sawtooth effect, 4–7, 42
scalability, 46, 148
scheduling, 50
scouting, 161–162, 177–194, 182–184.
  See also employees
self-confidence, 182
self-fulfilling prophecy, 15–16
skills, 182
  deficiencies in, 54
  development of employee, 187–191
  leadership, 32–33
  scouting for, 182–184
skunkworks, 165–166
smartphones, 135
Smith, Fred, 135–136, 151
sports, 178–179
stagnation, 7, 86
standardization, 74
standards
  articulating, 26
  attracting employees and, 177–179
  communicating, 26

standards (*continued*)
  for communication, 94
  leadership and, 30–31
  proactive improvements and,
    110–112, 121–122
  quality, 139–140
  raising the bar for, 38–44
  reliability, 139–140
  root causes of failure to meet,
    28–29
  teamwork and, 74–76
  what needs improvement, 48–49
  what went well, 48–49
start-ups, 113, 165–166
stewardship, 182
Stibich, Ron, 169–170
strategy, 155, 170–171
strengths, playing to, 190–191,
successes, learning from, 156–158
suppliers, 166–171, 173
support, 19–20
sure bets, 156–162
sustainability, 7
  high performers and, 43
  innovation and, 132–137
  quick wins and, 64–65
Switzler, Al, 197
systems
  developing, 35
  raising the bar and, 40–41
  unreliable, in Run-centric cultures,
    12–15

T
talent fleet. *See* employees
talent loss, 126
talents, 182
teams. *See also* employees
  building Grow, 177–194
  building with quick wins, 38,
    44–47

communication and, 74–76
customers in, 144–145
Grow, 166–171,
grow, 166–171
high performers and, 43
identifying strengths of, 191
integrated teamwork and, 75–76,
  84–85
management systems and, 83
momentum and, 77
proactive improvements and,
  121–122
stewardship of teamwork in, 183
superfluous systems and, 14
technology, 148
10-80-10
  attracting employees and, 180
  employee scouting and, 183–184
  reliability and quality and,
    139–140
  thought leaders/innovators and,
    119–121
thinking, shifting, 162, 163–164
thought leaders, 119–121
time management
  determining current time use and,
    4–10
  marathon managers and, 23–24
  proactive improvements and,
    114–115
  Run-Improve-Grow and, 7–10
  sawtooth effect and, 4–7
timing, 114
trade-offs, zero, 135–136
traffic cop management, 17–18
training, 44, 52–56
transformation, organizational,
  172–174
trend analysis, 161
trust, 26
  conveying in questions, 88
  dividends from, 35

lack of in Run-centric cultures, 10,
    11–12, 83–84
leadership and, 30–31
management systems and, 86–87
motivation and, 101–102
proactive improvement and, 115
quick wins and, 45
try-storming, 56
turf, protecting, 70
turnover, 184–185, 186

U
uncertainty, 113–114, 119–121, 138
United Parcel Service, 151
United States Postal Service (USPS),
    151
unreliability, 69–70
UPS, 151

V
value-added functions, 25. *See also*
    most-value-added (MVA)
    functions
value proposition, 9
Verizon, 139

visibility, of quick wins, 46
vision, 98–103, 115, 157
    attracting employees and, 180–181
    compromise and, 135–136
    Grow teams and, 168

W
Walt Disney Company, 131–132
waste, 136–137
"What if…?" questions, 123, 124–125
what needs improvement (WNI),
    48–49, 156
what went well (WWW), 48–49, 90,
    156
WNI. *See* what needs improvement
    (WNI)
WWW. *See* what went well
    (WWW)

Y
"Yes we can" discussions, 142–145

Z
zero trade-offs, 135–136, 152–153